International Code for the Construction and Equipment
of Ships Carrying Liquefied Gases in Bulk

IGC Code

1993 Edition

INTERNATIONAL
MARITIME
ORGANIZATION

London, 1993

Published in 1983
by the INTERNATIONAL MARITIME ORGANIZATION
4 Albert Embankment, London SE1 7SR
www.imo.org

Second edition, 1993

Printed in the United Kingdom by CPI Books Limited, Reading RG1 8EX

ISBN 978-92-801-1277-1

IMO PUBLICATION
Sales number: I104E

This publication has been prepared from official documents of IMO, and every effort has been made to eliminate errors and reproduce the original text(s) faithfully. Readers should be aware that, in case of inconsistency, the official IMO text will prevail.

K42136

Foreword

At its forty-eighth session (June 1983), the Maritime Safety Committee (MSC) of the International Maritime Organization (IMO) adopted far-reaching amendments to the International Convention for the Safety of Life at Sea (SOLAS), 1974, by resolution MSC.6(48).

The amendments consisted of complete replacement texts of chapters III and VII and changes in chapters II-1, II-2 and IV.

The new chapter VII made the provisions of the International Code for the Construction and Equipment of Ships Carrying Liquefied Gases in Bulk (IGC Code), which had been adopted by resolution MSC.5(48), mandatory under the 1974 SOLAS Convention.

The new 1993 edition of the IGC Code incorporates amendments adopted by the MSC at its sixty-first session (December 1992) by resolution MSC.30(61). These amendments will enter into force on 1 July 1994 once the procedures for acceptance have been fulfilled.

Contents

Chapter 4 – Cargo containment

Chapter 5 – Process pressure vessels and liquid, vapour and pressure piping systems

Chapter 6 – Materials of construction

Chapter 12 – Mechanical ventilation in the cargo area

Chapter 13 – Instrumentation (gauging, gas detection)

Chapter 14 – Personnel protection

Chapter 15 – Filling limits for cargo tanks

Chapter 16 – Use of cargo as fuel

Preamble

1   The purpose of this Code* is to provide an international standard for the safe carriage by sea in bulk of liquefied gases and certain other substances listed in chapter 19 of the Code, by prescribing the design and construction standards of ships involved in such carriage and the equipment they should carry so as to minimize the risk to the ship, to its crew and to the environment, having regard to the nature of the products involved.

2   The basic philosophy is one of ship types related to the hazards of the products covered by the Code. Each of the products may have one or more hazard properties which include flammability, toxicity, corrosivity and reactivity. A further possible hazard may arise due to the products being transported under cryogenic or pressure conditions.

3   Severe collisions or strandings could lead to cargo tank damage and result in uncontrolled release of the product. Such release could result in evaporation and dispersion of the product and, in some cases, could cause brittle fracture of the ship's hull. The requirements in the Code are intended to minimize this risk as far as is practicable, based upon present knowledge and technology.

4 Throughout the development of the Code it was recognized that it must be based upon sound naval architectural and engineering principles and the best understanding available as to the hazards of the various products covered; furthermore that gas carrier design technology is not only a complex technology but is rapidly evolving and that the Code should not remain static. Therefore the Organization will periodically review the Code taking into account both experience and future development.

5   Requirements for new products and their conditions of carriage will be circulated as recommendations, on an interim basis, when adopted by the Maritime Safety Committee of the Organization, prior to the entry into force of the appropriate amendments, under the terms of article VIII of the International Convention for the Safety of Life at Sea, 1974.

6   The Code primarily deals with ship design and equipment. In order to ensure the safe transport of the products the total system must, however, be appraised. Other important facets of the safe transport of the products, such as training, operation, traffic control and handling in port, are being or will be examined further by the Organization.

---

* The 1993 edition of the IGC Code comprises the annex to resolution MSC.5(48) and incorporates amendments adopted by resolution MSC.30(61). The latter resolution is shown on page 165.

7   The development of the Code has been greatly assisted by the work of the International Association of Classification Societies (IACS) and full account has been taken of the IACS Unified Requirements for Liquefied Gas Tankers in chapters 4, 5 and 6.

8   The relevant work of the International Electrotechnical Commission (IEC) has contributed substantially to the development of chapter 10.

9   Chapter 18 of the Code dealing with operation of liquefied gas carriers highlights the regulations in other chapters that are operational in nature and mentions those other important safety features that are peculiar to gas carrier operation.

10   The layout of the Code is in line with the International Code for the Construction and Equipment of Ships Carrying Dangerous Chemicals in Bulk (IBC Code) adopted by the Maritime Safety Committee at its forty-eighth session.

Chapter 1

General

1.1 Application

1.1.1 The Code applies to ships regardless of their size, including those of less than 500 tons gross tonnage, engaged in the carriage of liquefied gases having a vapour pressure exceeding 2.8 bar absolute at a temperature of 37.8°C, and other products as shown in chapter 19, when carried in bulk.

1.1.2 Unless expressly provided otherwise, the Code applies to ships the keels of which are laid or which are at a stage at which:

.1 construction identifiable with the ship begins; and

.2 assembly of that ship has commenced comprising at least 50 tonnes or 1% of the estimated mass of all structural material, whichever is less;

on or after 1 October 1994. Ships constructed before 1 October 1994 are to comply with resolution MSC.5(48) adopted on 17 June 1983.

1.1.3 A ship, irrespective of the date of construction, which is converted to a gas carrier on or after 1 July 1986, should be treated as a gas carrier constructed on the date on which such conversion commences.

1.1.4.1 When cargo tanks contain products for which the Code requires a type 1G ship, neither flammable liquids having a flashpoint of 60°C (closed cup test) or less nor flammable products listed in chapter 19 should be carried in tanks located within the protective zones described in 2.6.1.1.

1.1.4.2 Similarly, when cargo tanks contain products for which the Code requires a type 2G/2PG ship, the above-mentioned flammable liquids should not be carried in tanks located within the protective zones described in 2.6.1.2.

1.1.4.3 In each case the restriction applies to the protective zones within the longitudinal extent of the hold spaces for the cargo tanks loaded with products for which the Code requires a type 1G or 2G/2PG ship.

1.1.4.4 The above-mentioned flammable liquids and products may be carried within these protective zones when the quantity retained in the cargo tanks of products for which the Code requires a type 1G or 2G/2PG ship is solely used for cooling, circulation or fuelling purposes.

1.1.5 Except as provided in 1.1.7.1, when it is intended to carry products covered by this Code and products covered by the International Code for the Construction and Equipment of Ships Carrying Dangerous Chemicals in Bulk adopted by the Maritime Safety Committee under the authority of the Assembly of the Organization conferred by resolution A.490(XII), as may be amended by the Organization (IBC Code), the ship should comply with the requirements of both Codes appropriate to the products carried.

1.1.6 Where it is proposed to carry products which may be considered to come within the scope of the Code but are not at present designated in chapter 19, the Administrations and the port Administrations involved in such carriage should establish preliminary suitable conditions of carriage based on the principles of the Code and notify the Organization of such conditions.

1.1.7.1 The requirements of this Code should take precedence when a ship is designed and constructed for the carriage of the following products:

.1   those listed exclusively in chapter 19 of this Code; and

.2   one or more of the products which are listed both in this Code and in the International Bulk Chemical Code. These products are marked with an asterisk in column a in the table of chapter 19.

1.1.7.2 When a ship is intended exclusively to carry one or more of the products noted in 1.1.7.1.2, the requirements of the International Bulk Chemical Code as amended should apply.

1.1.8 Compliance of the ship with the requirements of the International Gas Carrier Code should be shown in the International Certificate of Fitness for the Carriage of Liquefied Gases in Bulk provided for in 1.5. Compliance with the amendments to the Code, as appropriate, should also be indicated in the International Certificate of Fitness for the Carriage of Liquefied Gases in Bulk.

1.2   Hazards

Hazards of gases considered in this Code include fire, toxicity, corrosivity, reactivity, low temperature and pressure.

1.3   Definitions

Except where expressly provided otherwise, the following definitions apply to the Code. Additional definitions are given in chapter 4.

1.3.1 *Accommodation spaces* are those spaces used for public spaces, corridors, lavatories, cabins, offices, hospitals, cinemas, games and hobbies rooms, barber shops, pantries containing no cooking appliances and similar spaces. Public spaces are those portions of the accommodation which are used for halls, dining rooms, lounges and similar permanently enclosed spaces.

1.3.2 *'A' class divisions* means divisions as defined in regulation II-2/3.3 of the 1983 SOLAS amendments.

1.3.3.1 *Administration* means the Government of the State whose flag the ship is entitled to fly.

1.3.3.2 *Port Administration* means the appropriate authority of the country in the port of which the ship is loading or unloading.

1.3.4 *Boiling point* is the temperature at which a product exhibits a vapour pressure equal to the atmospheric pressure.

1.3.5 *Breadth (B)* means the maximum breadth of the ship, measured amidships to the moulded line of the frame in a ship with a metal shell and to the outer surface of the hull in a ship with a shell of any other material. The breadth *(B)* should be measured in metres.

1.3.6 *Cargo area* is that part of the ship which contains the cargo containment system and cargo pump and compressor rooms and includes deck areas over the full length and breadth of the part of the ship over the above-mentioned spaces. Where fitted, the cofferdams, ballast or void spaces at the after end of the aftermost hold space or at the forward end of the forwardmost hold space are excluded from the cargo area.

1.3.7 *Cargo containment system* is the arrangement for containment of cargo including, where fitted, a primary and secondary barrier, associated insulation and any intervening spaces, and adjacent structure if necessary for the support of these elements. If the secondary barrier is part of the hull structure it may be a boundary of the hold space.

1.3.8 *Cargo control room* is a space used in the control of cargo handling operations and complying with the requirements of 3.4.

1.3.9 *Cargoes* are products listed in chapter 19 carried in bulk by ships subject to the Code.

1.3.10 *Cargo service spaces* are spaces within the cargo area used for workshops, lockers and store-rooms of more than 2 m² in area, used for cargo handling equipment.

1.3.11 *Cargo tank* is the liquid-tight shell designed to be the primary container of the cargo and includes all such containers whether or not associated with insulation or secondary barriers or both.

1.3.12 *Cofferdam* is the isolating space between two adjacent steel bulkheads or decks. This space may be a void space or a ballast space.

1.3.13 *Control stations* are those spaces in which ships' radio or main navigating equipment or the emergency source of power is located or where the fire-recording or fire control equipment is centralized. This does not include special fire control equipment which can be most practically located in the cargo area.

1.3.14 *Flammable products* are those identified by an F in column f in the table of chapter 19.

1.3.15 *Flammability limits* are the conditions defining the state of fuel-oxidant mixture at which application of an adequately strong external ignition source is only just capable of producing flammability in a given test apparatus.

1.3.16 *Gas carrier* is a cargo ship constructed or adapted and used for the carriage in bulk of any liquefied gas or other products listed in the table of chapter 19.

1.3.17 *Gas-dangerous space or zone* is:

   .1   a space in the cargo area which is not arranged or equipped in an approved manner to ensure that its atmosphere is at all times maintained in a gas-safe condition;

   .2   an enclosed space outside the cargo area through which any piping containing liquid or gaseous products passes, or within which such piping terminates, unless approved arrangements are installed to prevent any escape of product vapour into the atmosphere of that space;

   .3   a cargo containment system and cargo piping;

   .4.1   a hold space where cargo is carried in a cargo containment system requiring a secondary barrier;

   .4.2   a hold space where cargo is carried in a cargo containment system not requiring a secondary barrier;

   .5   a space separated from a hold space described in .4.1 by a single gastight steel boundary;

   .6   a cargo pump-room and cargo compressor room;

   .7   a zone on the open deck, or semi-enclosed space on the open deck, within 3 m of any cargo tank outlet, gas or vapour outlet, cargo pipe flange or cargo valve or of entrances and ventilation openings to cargo pump-rooms and cargo compressor rooms;

.8   the open deck over the cargo area and 3 m forward and aft of the cargo area on the open deck up to a height of 2.4 m above the weather deck;

.9   a zone within 2.4 m of the outer surface of a cargo containment system where such surface is exposed to the weather;

.10   an enclosed or semi-enclosed space in which pipes containing products are located. A space which contains gas detection equipment complying with 13.6.5 and a space utilizing boil-off gas as fuel and complying with chapter 16 are not considered gas-dangerous spaces in this context;

.11   a compartment for cargo hoses; or

.12   an enclosed or semi-enclosed space having a direct opening into any gas-dangerous space or zone.

1.3.18 *Gas-safe space* is a space other than a gas-dangerous space.

1.3.19 *Hold space* is the space enclosed by the ship's structure in which a cargo containment system is situated.

1.3.20 *Independent* means that a piping or venting system, for example, is in no way connected to another system and there are no provisions available for the potential connection to other systems.

1.3.21 *Insulation space* is the space, which may or may not be an interbarrier space, occupied wholly or in part by insulation.

1.3.22 *Interbarrier space* is the space between a primary and a secondary barrier, whether or not completely or partially occupied by insulation or other material.

1.3.23 *Length (L)* means 96% of the total length on a waterline at 85% of the least moulded depth measured from the top of the keel, or the length from the foreside of the stem to the axis of the rudder stock on that waterline, if that be greater. In ships designed with a rake of keel, the waterline on which this length is measured should be parallel to the designed waterline. The length *(L)* should be measured in metres.

1.3.24 *Machinery spaces of category A* are those spaces and trunks to such spaces which contain:

.1   internal combustion machinery used for main propulsion; or

.2   internal combustion machinery used for purposes other than main propulsion where such machinery has in the aggregate a total power output of not less than 375 kW; or

.3   any oil-fired boiler or oil fuel unit.

1.3.25 *Machinery spaces* are all machinery spaces of category A and all other spaces containing propelling machinery, boilers, oil fuel units, steam and internal combustion engines, generators and major electrical machinery, oil filling stations, refrigerating, stabilizing, ventilation and air-conditioning machinery, and similar spaces; and trunks to such spaces.

1.3.26 *MARVS* is the maximum allowable relief valve setting of a cargo tank.

1.3.27 *Oil fuel unit* is the equipment used for the preparation of oil fuel for delivery to an oil-fired boiler, or equipment used for the preparation for delivery of heated oil to an internal combustion engine, and includes any oil pressure pumps, filters and heaters dealing with oil at a pressure of more than 1.8 bar gauge.

1.3.28 *Organization* is the International Maritime Organization (IMO).

1.3.29 *Permeability* of a space means the ratio of the volume within that space which is assumed to be occupied by water to the total volume of that space.

1.3.30.1 *Primary barrier* is the inner element designed to contain the cargo when the cargo containment system includes two boundaries.

1.3.30.2 *Secondary barrier* is the liquid-resisting outer element of a cargo containment system designed to afford temporary containment of any envisaged leakage of liquid cargo through the primary barrier and to prevent the lowering of the temperature of the ship's structure to an unsafe level. Types of secondary barrier are more fully defined in chapter 4.

1.3.31 *Relative density* is the ratio of the mass of a volume of a product to the mass of an equal volume of fresh water.

1.3.32 *Separate* means that a cargo piping system or cargo vent system, for example, is not connected to another cargo piping or cargo vent system. This separation may be achieved by the use of design or operational methods. Operational methods should not be used within a cargo tank and should consist of one of the following types:

    .1   removing spool pieces or valves and blanking the pipe ends;

    .2   arrangement of two spectacle flanges in series with provisions for detecting leakage into the pipe between the two spectacle flanges.

1.3.33 *Service spaces* are those used for galleys, pantries containing cooking appliances, lockers, mail and specie rooms, store-rooms, workshops other than those forming part of the machinery spaces and similar spaces and trunks to such spaces.

1.3.34 *1974 SOLAS Convention* means the International Convention for the Safety of Life at Sea, 1974.

1.3.35 *1983 SOLAS amendments* means amendments to the 1974 SOLAS Convention adopted by the Maritime Safety Committee of the Organization at its forty-eighth session on 17 June 1983 by resolution MSC.6(48).

1.3.36 *Tank cover* is the protective structure intended to protect the cargo containment system against damage where it protrudes through the weather deck or to ensure the continuity and integrity of the deck structure.

1.3.37 *Tank dome* is the upward extension of a portion of a cargo tank. In the case of below-deck cargo containment systems the tank dome protrudes through the weather deck or through a tank cover.

1.3.38 *Toxic products* are those identified by a T in column f in the table of chapter 19.

1.3.39 *Vapour pressure* is the equilibrium pressure of the saturated vapour above the liquid expressed in bars absolute at a specified temperature.

1.3.40 *Void space* is an enclosed space in the cargo area external to a cargo containment system, other than a hold space, ballast space, fuel oil tank, cargo pump or compressor room, or any space in normal use by personnel.

1.4　Equivalents

1.4.1　Where the Code requires that a particular fitting, material, appliance, apparatus, item of equipment or type thereof should be fitted or carried in a ship, or that any particular provision should be made, or any procedure or arrangement should be complied with, the Administration may allow any other fitting, material, appliance, apparatus, item of equipment or type thereof to be fitted or carried, or any other provision, procedure or arrangement to be made in that ship, if it is satisfied by trial thereof or otherwise that such fitting, material, appliance, apparatus, item of equipment or type thereof or that any particular provision, procedure or arrangement is at least as effective as that required by the Code. However, the Administration may not allow operational methods or procedures to be made an alternative to a particular fitting, material, appliance, apparatus, item of equipment, or type thereof which is prescribed by the Code.

1.4.2　When the Administration so allows any fitting, material, appliance, apparatus, item of equipment, or type thereof, or provision, procedure or arrangement to be substituted, it should communicate to the Organization the particulars thereof together with a report on the evidence submitted, so that the Organization may circulate the same to other Contracting Governments to the 1974 SOLAS Convention for the information of their officers.

1.5 Surveys and certification

1.5.1 *Survey procedure*

1.5.1.1 The survey of ships, so far as regards the enforcement of the provisions of the regulations and the granting of exemptions therefrom, should be carried out by officers of the Administration. The Administration may, however, entrust the surveys either to surveyors nominated for the purpose or to organizations recognized by it.

1.5.1.2 The Administration nominating surveyors or recognizing organizations to conduct surveys should, as a minimum, empower any nominated surveyor or recognized organization to:

.1 require repairs to a ship; and

.2 carry out surveys if requested by the port State authority* concerned.

The Administration should notify the Organization of the specific responsibilities and conditions of the authority delegated to nominated surveyors or recognized organizations for circulation to the Contracting Governments.

1.5.1.3 When a nominated surveyor or recognized organization determines that the condition of the ship or its equipment does not correspond substantially with the particulars of the certificate or is such that the ship is not fit to proceed to sea without danger to the ship, or persons on board, such surveyor or organization should immediately ensure that corrective action is taken and should in due course notify the Administration. If such corrective action is not taken the relevant certificate should be withdrawn and the Administration should be notified immediately; and, if the ship is in a port of another Contracting Government, the port State authority concerned should also be notified immediately.

1.5.1.4 In every case, the Administration should guarantee the completeness and efficiency of the survey, and should undertake to ensure the necessary arrangements to satisfy this obligation.

1.5.2 *Survey requirements*

1.5.2.1 The structure, equipment, fittings, arrangements and material (other than items in respect of which a Cargo Ship Safety Construction Certificate,

---

* *Port State authority* has the meaning as presented in chapter I, regulation 19, of the 1978 Protocol to the 1974 SOLAS Convention.

Cargo Ship Safety Equipment Certificate and Cargo Ship Safety Radiotelegraphy Certificate or Cargo Ship Safety Radiotelephony Certificate is issued) of a gas carrier should be subjected to the following surveys:

.1 An initial survey before the ship is put in service or before the International Certificate of Fitness for the Carriage of Liquefied Gases in Bulk is issued for the first time, which should include a complete examination of its structure, equipment, fittings, arrangements and material in so far as the ship is covered by the Code. This survey should be such as to ensure that the structure, equipment, fittings, arrangements and material fully comply with the applicable provisions of the Code.

.2 A periodical survey at intervals specified by the Administration, but not exceeding five years which should be such as to ensure that the structure, equipment, fittings, arrangements and material comply with the applicable provisions of the Code.

.3 A minimum of one intermediate survey during the period of validity of the International Certificate of Fitness for the Carriage of Liquefied Gases in Bulk. In cases where only one such intermediate survey is carried out in any one certificate validity period, it should be held not before six months prior to, not later than six months after, the half-way date of the certificate's period of validity. Intermediate surveys should be such as to ensure that the safety equipment, and other equipment, and associated pump and piping systems comply with the applicable provisions of the Code and are in good working order. Such surveys should be endorsed on the International Certificate of Fitness for the Carriage of Liquefied Gases in Bulk.

.4 A mandatory annual survey within three months before or after the anniversary date of the International Certificate of Fitness for the Carriage of Liquefied Gases in Bulk which should include a general examination to ensure that the structure, equipment, fittings, arrangements and materials remain in all respects satisfactory for the service for which the ship is intended. Such a survey should be endorsed in the International Certificate of Fitness for the Carriage of Liquefied Gases in Bulk.

.5 An additional survey, either general or partial according to the circumstances, should be made when required after an investigation prescribed in 1.5.3.3, or whenever any important repairs or renewals are made. Such a survey should ensure that the necessary repairs or renewals have been effectively made, that the material and workmanship of such repairs or renewals are satisfactory; and that the ship is fit to proceed to sea without danger to the ship or persons on board.

1.5.3 *Maintenance of conditions after survey*

1.5.3.1 The condition of the ship and its equipment should be maintained to conform with the provisions of the Code to ensure that the ship will remain fit to proceed to sea without danger to the ship or persons on board.

1.5.3.2 After any survey of the ship under 1.5.2 has been completed, no change should be made in the structure, equipment, fittings, arrangements and material covered by the survey, without the sanction of the Administration, except by direct replacement.

1.5.3.3 Whenever an accident occurs to a ship or a defect is discovered, either of which affects the safety of the ship or the efficiency or completeness of its life-saving appliances or other equipment, the master or owner of the ship should report at the earliest opportunity to the Administration, the nominated surveyor or recognized organization responsible for issuing the relevant certificate, who should cause investigations to be initiated to determine whether a survey as required by 1.5.2.1.5 is necessary. If the ship is in a port of another Contracting Government, the master or owner should also report immediately to the port State authority concerned and the nominated surveyor or recognized organization should ascertain that such a report has been made.

1.5.4 *Issue of certificate*

1.5.4.1 A certificate called an International Certificate of Fitness for the Carriage of Liquefied Gases in Bulk, the model form of which is set out in the appendix, should be issued after an initial or periodical survey to a gas carrier which complies with the relevant requirements of the Code.

1.5.4.2 The certificate issued under the provisions of this section should be available on board for inspection at all times.

1.5.4.3 When a ship is designed and constructed under the provisions of 1.1.5, International Certificates of Fitness should be issued in accordance with the requirements of this section and with the requirements of section 1.5 of the International Bulk Chemical Code.

1.5.5 *Issue or endorsement of certificate by another Government*

1.5.5.1 A Contracting Government may, at the request of another Government, cause a ship entitled to fly the flag of the other State to be surveyed and, if satisfied that the requirements of the Code are complied with, issue or authorize the issue of the certificate to the ship, and, where appropriate, endorse or authorize the endorsement of the certificate on board the ship in accordance with the Code. Any certificate so issued should contain a statement to the effect that it has been issued at the request of the Government of the State whose flag the ship is entitled to fly.

1.5.6 *Duration and validity of the certificate*

1.5.6.1 An International Certificate of Fitness for the Carriage of Liquefied Gases in Bulk should be issued for a period specified by the Administration which should not exceed five years from the date of the initial survey or the periodical survey.

1.5.6.2 No extension of the five-year period of the certificate should be permitted.

1.5.6.3 The certificate should cease to be valid:

.1 if the surveys are not carried out within the period specified by 1.5.2;

.2 upon transfer of the ship to the flag of another State. A new certificate should only be issued when the Government issuing the new certificate is fully satisfied that the ship is in compliance with the requirements of 1.5.3.1 and 1.5.3.2. Where a transfer occurs between Contracting Governments, the Government of the State whose flag the ship was formerly entitled to fly should, if requested within 12 months after the transfer has taken place, as soon as possible transmit to the Administration copies of the certificates carried by the ship before the transfer and, if available, copies of the relevant survey reports.

Chapter 2

Ship survival capability*
and location of cargo tanks

2.1 General

2.1.1 Ships subject to the Code should survive the normal effects of flooding following assumed hull damage caused by some external force. In addition, to safeguard the ship and the environment, the cargo tanks should be protected from penetration in the case of minor damage to the ship resulting, for example, from contact with a jetty or tug, and given a measure of protection from damage in the case of collision or stranding, by locating them at specified minimum distances inboard from the ship's shell plating. Both the damage to be assumed and the proximity of the tanks to the ship's shell should be dependent upon the degree of hazard presented by the product to be carried.

2.1.2 Ships subject to the Code should be designed to one of the following standards:

.1 A *type 1G ship* is a gas carrier intended to transport products indicated in chapter 19 which require maximum preventive measures to preclude the escape of such cargo.

.2 A *type 2G ship* is a gas carrier intended to transport products indicated in chapter 19 which require significant preventive measures to preclude the escape of such cargo.

.3 A *type 2PG ship* is a gas carrier of 150 m in length or less intended to transport products indicated in chapter 19 which require significant preventive measures to preclude escape of such cargo, and where the products are carried in independent type C tanks designed (see 4.2.4.4) for a MARVS of at least 7 bar gauge and a cargo containment system design temperature of −55°C or above. Note that a ship of this description but over 150 m in length is to be considered a type 2G ship.

.4 A *type 3G ship* is a gas carrier intended to carry products indicated in chapter 19 which require moderate preventive measures to preclude the escape of such cargo.

Thus a type 1G ship is a gas carrier intended for the transportation of products considered to present the greatest overall hazard and types 2G/2PG

---

* Refer to the Guidelines for Uniform Application of the Survival Requirements of the Bulk Chemical Code and the Gas Carrier Code.

and type 3G for products of progressively lesser hazards. Accordingly, a type 1G ship should survive the most severe standard of damage and its cargo tanks should be located at the maximum prescribed distance inboard from the shell plating.

2.1.3 The ship type required for individual products is indicated in column c in the table of chapter 19.

2.1.4 If a ship is intended to carry more than one product listed in chapter 19, the standard of damage should correspond to that product having the most stringent ship type requirement. The requirements for the location of individual cargo tanks, however, are those for ship types related to the respective products intended to be carried.

2.2 Freeboard and intact stability

2.2.1 Ships subject to the Code may be assigned the minimum freeboard permitted by the International Convention on Load Lines in force. However, the draught associated with the assignment should not be greater than the maximum draught otherwise permitted by this Code.

2.2.2 The stability of the ship in all seagoing conditions and during loading and unloading cargo should be to a standard which is acceptable to the Administration.

2.2.3 When calculating the effect of free surfaces of consumable liquids for loading conditions it should be assumed that, for each type of liquid, at least one transverse pair or a single centre tank has a free surface and the tank or combination of tanks to be taken into account should be those where the effect of free surfaces is the greatest. The free surface effect in undamaged compartments should be calculated by a method acceptable to the Administration.

2.2.4 Solid ballast should not normally be used in double bottom spaces in the cargo area. Where, however, because of stability considerations, the fitting of solid ballast in such spaces becomes unavoidable, then its disposition should be governed by the need to ensure that the impact loads resulting from bottom damage are not directly transmitted to the cargo tank structure.

2.2.5 The master of the ship should be supplied with a loading and stability information booklet. This booklet should contain details of typical service conditions, loading, unloading and ballasting operations, provisions for evaluating other conditions of loading and a summary of the ship's survival capabilities. In addition, the booklet should contain sufficient information to enable the master to load and operate the ship in a safe and seaworthy manner.

2.3 Shipside discharges below the freeboard deck

2.3.1 The provision and control of valves fitted to discharges led through the shell from spaces below the freeboard deck or from within the superstructures and deck-houses on the freeboard deck fitted with weathertight doors should comply with the requirements of the relevant regulation of the International Convention on Load Lines in force, except that the choice of valves should be limited to:

- .1 one automatic nonreturn valve with a positive means of closing from above the freeboard deck; or

- .2 where the vertical distance from the summer load waterline to the inboard end of the discharge pipe exceeds 0.01L, two automatic nonreturn valves without positive means of closing, provided that the inboard valve is always accessible for examination under service conditions.

2.3.2 For the purpose of this chapter, *summer load waterline* and *freeboard deck* have the meanings defined in the International Convention on Load Lines in force.

2.3.3 The automatic nonreturn valves referred to in 2.3.1.1 and 2.3.1.2 should be of a type acceptable to the Administration and should be fully effective in preventing admission of water into the ship, taking into account the sinkage, trim and heel in survival requirements in 2.9.

2.4 Conditions of loading

Damage survival capability should be investigated on the basis of loading information submitted to the Administration for all anticipated conditions of loading and variations in draught and trim. The survival requirements need not be applied to the ship when in the ballast condition,* provided that any cargo retained on board is solely used for cooling, circulation or fuelling purposes.

2.5 Damage assumptions

2.5.1 The assumed maximum extent of damage should be:

- .1 Side damage:

- .1.1 Longitudinal extent: 1/3$L^{2/3}$ or 14.5 m, whichever is less

---

* The cargo content of small independent purge tanks on deck need not be taken into account when assessing the ballast condition.

			For 0.3L from the forward perpendicular of the ship	Any other part of the ship

.1.2 Transverse extent: measured inboard from the ship's side at right angles to the centreline at the level of the summer load line — $B/5$ or 11.5 m, whichever is less

.1.3 Vertical extent: from the moulded line of the bottom shell plating at centreline — upwards without limit

.2 Bottom damage:

	For 0.3L from the forward perpendicular of the ship	Any other part of the ship
.2.1 Longitudinal extent:	$1/3L^{2/3}$ or 14.5 m, whichever is less	$1/3L^{2/3}$ or 5 m, whichever is less
.2.2 Transverse extent:	$B/6$ or 10 m, whichever is less	$B/6$ or 5 m, whichever is less
.2.3 Vertical extent:	$B/15$ or 2 m, whichever is less measured from the moulded line of the bottom shell plating at centreline (see 2.6.3).	$B/15$ or 2 m, whichever is less measured from the moulded line of the bottom shell plating at centreline (see 2.6.3).

2.5.2 Other damage:

.1 If any damage of a lesser extent than the maximum damage specified in 2.5.1 would result in a more severe condition, such damage should be assumed.

.2 Local side damage anywhere in the cargo area extending inboard 760 mm measured normal to the hull shell should be considered and transverse bulkheads should be assumed damaged when also required by the applicable subparagraphs of 2.8.1.

2.6 Location of cargo tanks

2.6.1 Cargo tanks should be located at the following distances inboard:

.1 Type 1G ships: from the side shell plating not less than the transverse extent of damage specified in 2.5.1.1.2 and from the moulded line of the bottom shell plating at centreline not less than the vertical extent of damage specified in 2.5.1.2.3 and nowhere less than 760 mm from the shell plating.

.2 Types 2G/2PG and 3G ships: from the moulded line of the bottom shell plating at centreline not less than the vertical extent of damage specified in 2.5.1.2.3 and nowhere less than 760 mm from the shell plating.

2.6.2 For the purpose of tank location, the vertical extent of bottom damage should be measured to the inner bottom when membrane or semi-membrane tanks are used, otherwise to the bottom of the cargo tanks. The transverse extent of side damage should be measured to the longitudinal bulkhead when membrane or semi-membrane tanks are used, otherwise to the side of the cargo tanks (see figure 2.1). For internal insulation tanks the extent of damage should be measured to the supporting tank plating.

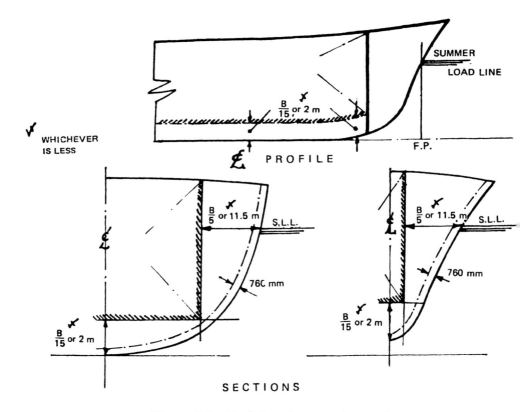

Figure 2.1 – *Tank location requirements*

2.6.3 Except for type 1G ships, suction wells installed in cargo tanks may protrude into the vertical extent of bottom damage specified in 2.5.1.2.3 provided that such wells are as small as practicable and the protrusion below the inner bottom plating does not exceed 25% of the depth of the double bottom or 350 mm, whichever is less. Where there is no double bottom, the protrusion below the upper limit of bottom damage should not exceed 350 mm. Suction wells installed in accordance with this paragraph may be ignored in determining the compartments affected by damage.

2.7 Flooding assumptions

2.7.1 The requirements of 2.9 should be confirmed by calculations which take into consideration the design characteristics of the ship; the arrangements, configuration and contents of the damaged compartments; the distribution, relative densities and the free surface effects of liquids; and the draught and trim for all conditions of loading.

2.7.2 The permeabilities of spaces assumed to be damaged should be as follows:

Spaces	Permeabilities
Appropriated to stores	0.60
Occupied by accommodation	0.95
Occupied by machinery	0.85
Voids	0.95
Intended for consumable liquids	0 to 0.95*
Intended for other liquids	0 to 0.95*

2.7.3 Wherever damage penetrates a tank containing liquids, it should be assumed that the contents are completely lost from that compartment and replaced by salt water up to the level of the final plane of equilibrium.

2.7.4 Where the damage between transverse watertight bulkheads is envisaged as specified in 2.8.1.4, .5, and .6, transverse bulkheads should be spaced at least at a distance equal to the longitudinal extent of damage specified in 2.5.1.1.1 in order to be considered effective. Where transverse bulkheads are spaced at a lesser distance, one or more of these bulkheads within such extent of damage should be assumed as non-existent for the purpose of determining flooded compartments. Further, any portion of a

---

* The permeability of partially filled compartments should be consistent with the amount of liquid carried in the compartment.

transverse bulkhead bounding side compartments or double bottom compartments should be assumed damaged if the watertight bulkhead boundaries are within the extent of vertical or horizontal penetration required by 2.5. Also, any transverse bulkhead should be assumed damaged if it contains a step or recess of more than 3 m in length located within the extent of penetration of assumed damage. The step formed by the after peak bulkhead and after peak tank top should not be regarded as a step for the purpose of this paragraph.

2.7.5 The ship should be so designed as to keep unsymmetrical flooding to the minimum consistent with efficient arrangements.

2.7.6 Equalization arrangements requiring mechanical aids such as valves or cross-levelling pipes, if fitted, should not be considered for the purpose of reducing an angle of heel or attaining the minimum range of residual stability to meet the requirements of 2.9.1 and sufficient residual stability should be maintained during all stages where equalization is used. Spaces which are linked by ducts of large cross-sectional area may be considered to be common.

2.7.7 If pipes, ducts, trunks or tunnels are situated within the assumed extent of damage penetration, as defined in 2.5, arrangements should be such that progressive flooding cannot thereby extend to compartments other than those assumed to be flooded for each case of damage.

2.7.8 The buoyancy of any superstructure directly above the side damage should be disregarded. The unflooded parts of superstructures beyond the extent of damage, however, may be taken into consideration provided that:

.1 they are separated from the damaged space by watertight divisions and the requirements of 2.9.1.1 in respect of these intact spaces are complied with; and

.2 openings in such divisions are capable of being closed by remotely operated sliding watertight doors and unprotected openings are not immersed within the minimum range of residual stability required in 2.9.2.1; however the immersion of any other openings capable of being closed weathertight may be permitted.

2.8 Standard of damage

2.8.1 Ships should be capable of surviving the damage indicated in 2.5 with the flooding assumptions in 2.7 to the extent determined by the ship's type according to the following standards:

.1 A type 1G ship should be assumed to sustain damage anywhere in its length;

.2 A type 2G ship of more than 150 m in length should be assumed to sustain damage anywhere in its length;

.3   A type 2G ship of 150 m in length or less should be assumed to sustain damage anywhere in its length except involving either of the bulkheads bounding a machinery space located aft;

.4   A type 2PG ship should be assumed to sustain damage anywhere in its length except involving transverse bulkheads spaced further apart than the longitudinal extent of damage as specified in 2.5.1.1.1;

.5   A type 3G ship of 125 m in length or more should be assumed to sustain damage anywhere in its length except involving transverse bulkheads spaced further apart than the longitudinal extent of damage specified in 2.5.1.1.1;

.6   A type 3G ship less than 125 m in length should be assumed to sustain damage anywhere in its length except involving transverse bulkheads spaced further apart than the longitudinal extent of damaged specified in 2.5.1.1.1 and except damage involving the machinery space when located aft. However, the ability to survive the flooding of the machinery space should be considered by the Administration.

2.8.2 In the case of small type 2G/2PG and 3G ships which do not comply in all respects with the appropriate requirements of 2.8.1.3, .4, and .6, special dispensations may only be considered by the Administration provided that alternative measures can be taken which maintain the same degree of safety. The nature of the alternative measures should be approved and clearly stated and be available to the port Administration. Any such dispensation should be duly noted on the International Certificate of Fitness for the Carriage of Liquefied Gases in Bulk referred to in 1.5.4.

2.9   Survival requirements

Ships subject to the Code should be capable of surviving the assumed damage specified in 2.5 to the standard provided in 2.8 in a condition of stable equilibrium and should satisfy the following criteria.

2.9.1 In any stage of flooding:

.1   the waterline, taking into account sinkage, heel and trim, should be below the lower edge of any opening through which progressive flooding or downflooding may take place. Such openings should include air pipes and openings which are closed by means of weathertight doors or hatch covers and may exclude those openings closed by means of watertight manhole covers and watertight flush scuttles, small watertight cargo tank hatch covers which maintain the high integrity of the deck, remotely operated watertight sliding doors, and sidescuttles of the non-opening type;

.2　the maximum angle of heel due to unsymmetrical flooding should not exceed 30°; and

.3　the residual stability during intermediate stages of flooding should be to the satisfaction of the Administration. However, it should never be significantly less than that required by 2.9.2.1.

2.9.2 At final equilibrium after flooding:

.1　the righting lever curve should have a minimum range of 20° beyond the position of equilibrium in association with a maximum residual righting lever of at least 0.1 m within the 20° range; the area under the curve within this range should not be less than 0.0175 m.rad. Unprotected openings should not be immersed within this range unless the space concerned is assumed to be flooded. Within this range, the immersion of any of the openings listed in 2.9.1.1 and other openings capable of being closed weathertight may be permitted; and

.2　the emergency source of power should be capable of operating.

Chapter 3

Ship arrangements

3.1 Segregation of the cargo area

3.1.1 Hold spaces should be segregated from machinery and boiler spaces, accommodation spaces, service spaces and control stations, chain lockers, drinking and domestic water tanks and from stores. Hold spaces should be located forward of machinery spaces of category A, other than those deemed necessary by the Administration for the safety or navigation of the ship.

3.1.2 Where cargo is carried in a cargo containment system not requiring a secondary barrier, segregation of hold spaces from spaces referred to in 3.1.1 or spaces either below or outboard of the hold spaces may be effected by cofferdams, fuel oil tanks or a single gastight bulkhead of all-welded construction forming an A-60 class division. A gastight A-0 class division is satisfactory if there is no source of ignition or fire hazard in the adjoining spaces.

3.1.3 Where cargo is carried in a cargo containment system requiring a secondary barrier, segregation of hold spaces from spaces referred to in 3.1.1 or spaces either below or outboard of the hold spaces which contain a source of ignition or fire hazard should be effected by cofferdams or fuel oil tanks. If there is no source of ignition or fire hazard in the adjoining space, segregation may be by a single A-0 class division which is gastight.

3.1.4 When cargo is carried in a cargo containment system requiring a secondary barrier:

.1 at temperatures below −10°C, hold spaces should be segregated from the sea by a double bottom; and

.2 at temperatures below −55°C, the ship should also have a longitudinal bulkhead forming side tanks.

3.1.5 Any piping system which may contain cargo or cargo vapour should:

.1 be segregated from other piping systems, except where interconnections are required for cargo-related operations such as purging, gas-freeing or inerting. In such cases, precautions should be taken to ensure that cargo or cargo vapour cannot enter such other piping systems through the interconnections;

.2 except as provided in chapter 16, not pass through any accommodation space, service space or control station or through a machinery space other than a cargo pump-room or cargo compressor space;

.3 be connected into the cargo containment system directly from the open deck except that pipes installed in a vertical trunkway or equivalent may be used to traverse void spaces above a cargo containment system and except that pipes for drainage, venting or purging may traverse cofferdams;

.4 except for bow or stern loading and unloading arrangements in accordance with 3.8 and emergency cargo jettisoning piping systems in accordance with 3.1.6, and except in accordance with chapter 16, be located in the cargo area above the open deck; and

.5 except for thwartship shore connection piping not subject to internal pressure at sea or emergency cargo jettisoning piping systems, be located inboard of the transverse tank location requirements of 2.6.1.

3.1.6 Any emergency cargo jettisoning piping system should comply with 3.1.5 as appropriate and may be led aft externally to accommodation spaces, service spaces or control stations or machinery spaces, but should not pass through them. If an emergency cargo jettisoning piping system is permanently installed, a suitable means of isolation from the cargo piping should be provided within the cargo area.

3.1.7 Arrangements should be made for sealing the weather decks in way of openings for cargo containment systems.

3.2 Accommodation, service and machinery spaces and control stations

3.2.1 No accommodation space, service space or control station should be located within the cargo area. The bulkhead of accommodation spaces, service spaces or control stations which face the cargo area should be so located as to avoid the entry of gas from the hold space to such spaces through a single failure of a deck or bulkhead on a ship having a containment system requiring a secondary barrier.

3.2.2 In order to guard against the danger of hazardous vapours, due consideration should be given to the location of air intakes and openings into accommodation, service and machinery spaces and control stations in relation to cargo piping, cargo vent systems and machinery space exhausts from gas burning arrangements.

3.2.3 Access through doors, gastight or otherwise, should not be permitted from a gas-safe space to a gas-dangerous space, except for access to service spaces forward of the cargo area through airlocks as permitted by 3.6.1 when accommodation spaces are aft.

3.2.4 Entrances, air inlets and openings to accommodation spaces, service spaces, machinery spaces and control stations should not face the cargo area. They should be located on the end bulkhead not facing the cargo area or on the outboard side of the superstructure or deck-house or on both at a distance of at least 4% of the length (L) of the ship but not less than 3 m from the end of the superstructure or deck-house facing the cargo area. This distance, however, need not exceed 5 m. Windows and sidescuttles facing the cargo area and on the sides of the superstructures or deck-houses within the distance mentioned above should be of the fixed (non-opening) type. Wheelhouse windows may be non-fixed and wheelhouse doors may be located within the above limits so long as they are so designed that a rapid and efficient gas and vapour tightening of the wheelhouse can be ensured. For ships dedicated to the carriage of cargoes which have neither flammable nor toxic hazards, the Administration may approve relaxations from the above requirements.

3.2.5 Sidescuttles in the shell below the uppermost continuous deck and in the first tier of the superstructure or deck-house should be of the fixed (non-opening) type.

3.2.6 All air intakes and openings into the accommodation spaces, service spaces and control stations should be fitted with closing devices. For toxic gases they should be operated from inside the space.

3.3   Cargo pump-rooms and cargo compressor rooms

3.3.1.1 Cargo pump-rooms and cargo compressor rooms should be situated above the weather deck and located within the cargo area unless specially approved by the Administration. Cargo compressor rooms should be treated as cargo pump-rooms for the purpose of fire protection according to regulation II-2/58 of the 1983 SOLAS amendments.

3.3.1.2 When cargo pump-rooms and cargo compressor rooms are permitted to be fitted above or below the weather deck at the after end of the aftermost hold space or at the forward end of the forwardmost hold space, the limits of the cargo area as defined in 1.3.6 should be extended to include the cargo pump-rooms and cargo compressor rooms for the full breadth and depth of the ship and deck areas above those spaces.

3.3.1.3 Where the limits of the cargo area are extended by 3.3.1.2, the bulkhead which separates the cargo pump-rooms and cargo compressor rooms from accommodation and service spaces, control stations and machinery spaces of category A should be so located as to avoid the entry of gas to these spaces through a single failure of a deck or bulkhead.

3.3.2 Where pumps and compressors are driven by shafting passing through a bulkhead or deck, gastight seals with efficient lubrication or other means of ensuring the permanence of the gas seal should be fitted in way of the bulkhead or deck.

3.3.3 Arrangements of cargo pump-rooms and cargo compressor rooms should be such as to ensure safe unrestricted access for personnel wearing protective clothing and breathing apparatus, and in the event of injury to allow unconscious personnel to be removed. All valves necessary for cargo handling should be readily accessible to personnel wearing protective clothing. Suitable arrangements should be made to deal with drainage of pump and compressor rooms.

3.4 Cargo control rooms

3.4.1 Any cargo control room should be above the weather deck and may be located in the cargo area. The cargo control room may be located within the accommodation spaces, service spaces or control stations provided the following conditions are complied with:

.1 the cargo control room is a gas-safe space; and

.2.1 if the entrance complies with 3.2.4, the control room may have access to the spaces described above;

.2.2 if the entrance does not comply with 3.2.4, the control room should have no access to the spaces described above and the boundaries to such spaces should be insulated to A-60 class integrity.

3.4.2 If the cargo control room is designed to be a gas-safe space, instrumentation should, as far as possible, be by indirect reading systems and should in any case be designed to prevent any escape of gas into the atmosphere of that space. Location of the gas detector within the cargo control room will not violate the gas-safe space if installed in accordance with 13.6.5.

3.4.3 If the cargo control room for ships carrying flammable cargoes is a gas-dangerous space, sources of ignition should be excluded. Consideration should be paid to the safety characteristics of any electrical installations.

3.5 Access to spaces in the cargo area

3.5.1 Visual inspection should be possible of at least one side of the inner hull structure without the removal of any fixed structure or fitting. If such a visual inspection, whether combined with those inspections required in 3.5.2, 4.7.7 or 4.10.16 or not, is only possible at the outer face of the inner hull, the inner hull should not be a fuel-oil tank boundary wall.

3.5.2 Inspection of one side of any insulation in hold spaces should be possible. If the integrity of the insulation system can be verified by inspection of the outside of the hold space boundary when tanks are at service temperature, inspection of one side of the insulation in the hold space need not be required.

3.5.3 Arrangements for hold spaces, void spaces and other spaces that could be considered gas-dangerous and cargo tanks should be such as to allow entry and inspection of any such space by personnel wearing protective clothing and breathing apparatus and in the event of injury to allow unconscious personnel to be removed from the space and should comply with the following:

.1 Access should be provided:

.1.1 to cargo tanks direct from the open deck;

.1.2 through horizontal openings, hatches or manholes, the dimensions of which should be sufficient to allow a person wearing a breathing apparatus to ascend or descend any ladder without obstruction and also to provide a clear opening to facilitate the hoisting of an injured person from the bottom of the space; the minimum clear opening should be not less than 600 mm × 600 mm; and

.1.3 through vertical openings, or manholes providing passage through the length and breadth of the space, the minimum clear opening of which should be not less than 600 mm × 800 mm at a height of not more than 600 mm from the bottom plating unless gratings or other footholds are provided.

.2 The dimensions referred to in 3.5.3.1.2 and .1.3 may be decreased if the ability to traverse such openings or to remove an injured person can be proved to the satisfaction of the Administration.

.3 The requirements of 3.5.3.1.2 and .1.3 do not apply to spaces described in 1.3.17.5. Such spaces should be provided only with direct or indirect access from the open weather deck, not including an enclosed gas-safe space.

3.5.4 Access from the open weather deck to gas-safe spaces should be located in a gas-safe zone at least 2.4 m above the weather deck unless the access is by means of· an airlock in accordance with 3.6.

3.6 Airlocks

3.6.1 An airlock should only be permitted between a gas-dangerous zone on the open weather deck and a gas-safe space and should consist of two steel doors substantially gastight spaced as least 1.5 m but not more than 2.5 m apart.

3.6.2 The doors should be self-closing and without any holding back arrangements.

3.6.3 An audible and visual alarm system to give a warning on both sides of the airlock should be provided to indicate if more than one door is moved from the closed position.

3.6.4 In ships carrying flammable products, electrical equipment which is not of the certified safe type in spaces protected by airlocks should be de-energized upon loss of overpressure in the space (see also 10.2.5.4). Electrical equipment which is not of the certified safe type for manoeuvring, anchoring and mooring equipment as well as the emergency fire pumps should not be located in spaces to be protected by airlocks.

3.6.5 The airlock space should be mechanically ventilated from a gas-safe space and maintained at an overpressure to the gas-dangerous zone on the open weather deck.

3.6.6 The airlock space should be monitored for cargo vapour.

3.6.7 Subject to the requirements of the International Convention on Load Lines in force, the door sill should not be less than 300 mm in height.

3.7 Bilge, ballast and fuel oil arrangements

3.7.1.1 Where cargo is carried in a cargo containment system not requiring a secondary barrier, hold spaces should be provided with suitable drainage arrangements not connected with the machinery space. Means of detecting any leakage should be provided.

3.7.1.2 Where there is a secondary barrier, suitable drainage arrangements for dealing with any leakage into the hold or insulation spaces through adjacent ship structure should be provided. The suction should not be led to pumps inside the machinery space. Means of detecting such leakage should be provided.

3.7.2 The interbarrier space should be provided with a drainage system suitable for handling liquid cargo in the event of cargo tank leakage or rupture. Such arrangements should provide for the return of leakage to the cargo tanks.

3.7.3 In case of internal insulation tanks, means of detecting leakage and drainage arrangements are not required for interbarrier spaces and spaces between the secondary barrier and the inner hull or independent tank structure which are completely filled by insulation material complying with 4.9.7.2.

3.7.4 Ballast spaces, fuel oil tanks and gas-safe spaces may be connected to pumps in the machinery spaces. Duct keels may be connected to pumps in the machinery spaces, provided the connections are led directly to the pumps and the discharge from the pumps led directly overboard with no valves or manifolds in either line which could connect the line from the duct keel to lines serving gas-safe spaces. Pump vents should not be open to machinery spaces.

3.8 Bow or stern loading and unloading arrangements

3.8.1 Subject to the approval of the Administration and to the requirements of this section, cargo piping may be arranged to permit bow or stern loading and unloading.

3.8.1.1 Bow or stern loading and unloading lines which are led past accommodation spaces, service spaces or control stations should not be used for the transfer of products requiring a type 1G ship. Bow or stern loading and unloading lines should not be used for the transfer of toxic products as specified in 1.3.38 unless specifically approved by the Administration.

3.8.2 Portable arrangements should not be permitted.

3.8.3 In addition to the requirements of chapter 5 the following provisions apply to cargo piping and related piping equipment:

.1 Cargo piping and related piping equipment outside the cargo area should have only welded connections. The piping outside the cargo area should run on the open deck and should be at least 760 mm inboard except for thwartships shore connection piping. Such piping should be clearly identified and fitted with a shutoff valve at its connection to the cargo piping system within the cargo area. At this location, it should also be capable of being separated by means of a removable spool piece and blank flanges when not in use.

.2 The piping is to be full penetration butt welded, and fully radiographed regardless of pipe diameter and design temperature. Flange connections in the piping are only permitted within the cargo area and at the shore connection.

.3 Arrangements should be made to allow such piping to be purged and gas-freed after use. When not in use, the spool pieces should be removed and the pipe ends be blank-flanged. The vent pipes connected with the purge should be located in the cargo area.

3.8.4 Entrances, air inlets and openings to accommodation spaces, service spaces, machinery spaces and control stations should not face the cargo shore connection location of bow or stern loading and unloading arrangements. They should be located on the outboard side of the superstructure or deck-house at a distance of at least 4% of the length of the ship but not less than 3 m from the end of the superstructure or deck-house facing the cargo shore connection location of the bow or stern loading and unloading arrangements. This distance, however, need not exceed 5 m. Sidescuttles facing the shore connection location and on the sides of the superstructure or deck-house within the distance mentioned above should be of the fixed (non-opening) type. In addition, during the use of the bow or stern loading and unloading arrangements, all doors, ports and other openings on the corresponding superstructure or deck-house side should be kept closed. Where, in the case of small ships, compliance with 3.2.4 and this paragraph is not possible, the Administration may approve relaxations from the above requirements.

3.8.5 Deck openings and air inlets to spaces within distances of 10 m from the cargo shore connection location should be kept closed during the use of bow or stern loading or unloading arrangements.

3.8.6 Electrical equipment within a zone of 3 m from the cargo shore connection location should be in accordance with chapter 10.

3.8.7 Fire-fighting arrangements for the bow or stern loading and unloading areas should be in accordance with 11.3.1.3 and 11.4.7.

3.8.8 Means of communication between the cargo control station and the shore connection location should be provided and if necessary certified safe.

Chapter 4

Cargo containment

4.1 General

4.1.1 Administrations should take appropriate steps to ensure uniformity in the implementation and application of the provisions of this chapter.*

4.1.2 In addition to the definitions in 1.3, the definitions given in this chapter apply throughout the Code.

4.2 Definitions

4.2.1 *Integral tanks*

4.2.1.1 Integral tanks form a structural part of the ship's hull and are influenced in the same manner and by the same loads which stress the adjacent hull structure.

4.2.1.2 The design vapour pressure P_o as defined in 4.2.6 should not normally exceed 0.25 bar. If, however, the hull scantlings are increased accordingly, P_o may be increased to a higher value but less than 0.7 bar.

4.2.1.3 Integral tanks may be used for products provided the boiling point of the cargo is not below −10°C. A lower temperature may be accepted by the Administration subject to special consideration.

4.2.2 *Membrane tanks*

4.2.2.1 Membrane tanks are non-self-supporting tanks which consist of a thin layer (membrane) supported through insulation by the adjacent hull structure. The membrane is designed in such a way that thermal and other expansion or contraction is compensated for without undue stressing of the membrane.

4.2.2.2 The design vapour pressure P_o should not normally exceed 0.25 bar. If, however, the hull scantlings are increased accordingly and consideration is given, where appropriate, to the strength of the supporting insulation, P_o may be increased to a higher value but less than 0.7 bar.

---

* Refer to the published Rules of members and associate members of the International Association of Classification Societies and in particular to *IACS Unified Requirements Nos. G1 and G2.*

4.2.2.3 The definition of membrane tanks does not exclude designs such as those in which nonmetallic membranes are used or in which membranes are included or incorporated in insulation. Such designs require, however, special consideration by the Administration. In any case the thickness of the membranes should normally not exceed 10 mm.

4.2.3 Semi-membrane tanks

4.2.3.1 Semi-membrane tanks are non-self-supporting tanks in the loaded condition and consist of a layer, parts of which are supported through insulation by the adjacent hull structure, whereas the rounded parts of this layer connecting the above-mentioned supported parts are designed also to accommodate the thermal and other expansion or contraction.

4.2.3.2 The design vapour pressure P_o should not normally exceed 0.25 bar. If, however, the hull scantlings are increased accordingly and consideration is given, where appropriate, to the strength of the supporting insulation, P_o may be increased to a higher value but less than 0.7 bar.

4.2.4 Independent tanks

4.2.4.1 Independent tanks are self-supporting; they do not form part of the ship's hull and are not essential to the hull strength. There are three categories of independent tanks referred to in 4.2.4.2 to 4.2.4.4.

4.2.4.2 Type A independent tanks are tanks which are designed primarily using Recognized Standards* of classical ship-structural analysis procedures. Where such tanks are primarily constructed of plane surfaces (gravity tanks), the design vapour pressure P_o should be less than 0.7 bar.

4.2.4.3 Type B independent tanks are tanks which are designed using model tests, refined analytical tools and analysis methods to determine stress levels, fatigue life and crack propagation characteristics. Where such tanks are primarily constructed of plane surfaces (gravity tanks) the design vapour pressure P_o should be less than 0.7 bar.

4.2.4.4 Type C independent tanks (also referred to as pressure vessels) are tanks meeting pressure vessel criteria and having a design vapour pressure not less than:

$$P_o = 2 + AC(\rho_r)^{1.5} \quad \text{(bar)}$$

where:

$$A = 0.0185 \left(\frac{\sigma_m}{\Delta \sigma_A} \right)^2$$

---

* *Recognized Standards* for the purpose of chapters 4, 5 and 6 are standards laid down and maintained by a classification society recognized by the Administration.

with

σ_m = design primary membrane stress

$\Delta\sigma_A$ = allowable dynamic membrane stress (double amplitude at probability level $Q = 10^{-8}$)
55 N/mm² for ferritic/martensitic steel
25 N/mm² for aluminium alloy (5083-0)

C = a characteristic tank dimension to be taken as the greatest of the following:

h, $0.75b$ or 0.45ℓ

with

h = height of tank (dimension in ship's vertical direction) (m)

b = width of tank (dimension in ship's transverse direction) (m)

ℓ = length of tank (dimension in ship's longitudinal direction) (m)

ρ_r = the relative density of the cargo ($\rho_r = 1$ for fresh water) at the design temperature.

However, the Administration may allocate a tank complying with the criterion of this subparagraph to type A or type B, dependent on the configuration of the tank and the arrangement of its supports and attachments.

4.2.5 Internal insulation tanks

4.2.5.1 Internal insulation tanks are non-self-supporting and consist of thermal insulation materials which contribute to the cargo containment and are supported by the structure of the adjacent inner hull or of an independent tank. The inner surface of the insulation is exposed to the cargo.

4.2.5.2 The two categories of internal insulation tanks are:

.1 Type 1 tanks, which are tanks in which the insulation or a combination of the insulation and one or more liners functions only as the primary barrier. The inner hull or an independent tank structure should function as the secondary barrier when required.

.2 Type 2 tanks, which are tanks in which the insulation or a combination of the insulation and one or more liners functions as both the primary and the secondary barrier and where these barriers are clearly distinguishable.

The term *liner* means a thin, non-self-supporting, metallic, nonmetallic or composite material which forms part of an internal insulation tank in order to enhance its fracture resistance or other mechanical properties. A liner differs from a membrane in that it is not intended to function alone as a liquid barrier.

4.2.5.3 Internal insulation tanks should be of suitable materials enabling the cargo containment system to be designed using model tests and refined analytical methods as required in 4.4.7.

4.2.5.4 The design vapour pressure P_o should not normally exceed 0.25 bar. If, however, the cargo containment system is designed for a higher vapour pressure, P_o may be increased to such higher value, but not exceeding 0.7 bar if the internal insulation tanks are supported by the inner hull structure. However, a design vapour pressure of more than 0.7 bar may be accepted by the Administration provided the internal insulation tanks are supported by suitable independent tank structures.

4.2.6 Design vapour pressure

4.2.6.1 The design vapour pressure P_o is the maximum gauge pressure at the top of the tank which has been used in the design of the tank.

4.2.6.2 For cargo tanks where there is no temperature control and where the pressure of the cargo is dictated only by the ambient temperature, P_o should not be less than the gauge vapour pressure of the cargo at a temperature of 45°C. However, lesser values of this temperature may be accepted by the Administration for ships operating in restricted areas or on voyages of restricted duration and account may be taken in such cases of any insulation of the tanks. Conversely, higher values of this temperature may be required for ships permanently operating in areas of high ambient temperature.

4.2.6.3 In all cases, including 4.2.6.2, P_o should not be less than MARVS.

4.2.6.4 Subject to special consideration by the Administration and to the limitations given in 4.2.1 to 4.2.5 for the various tank types, a vapour pressure higher than P_o may be accepted in harbour conditions, where dynamic loads are reduced.

4.2.7 Design temperature

The design temperature for selection of materials is the minimum temperature at which cargo may be loaded or transported in the cargo tanks. Provision to the satisfaction of the Administration should be made to ensure that the tank or cargo temperature cannot be lowered below the design temperature.

4.3 Design loads

4.3.1 *General*

4.3.1.1 Tanks together with their supports and other fixtures should be designed taking into account proper combinations of the following loads:

- internal pressure
- external pressure
- dynamic loads due to the motions of the ship
- thermal loads
- sloshing loads
- loads corresponding to ship deflection
- tank and cargo weight with the corresponding reactions in way of supports
- insulation weight
- loads in way of towers and other attachments.

The extent to which these loads should be considered depends on the type of tank, and is more fully detailed in the following paragraphs.

4.3.1.2 Account should be taken of the loads corresponding to the pressure test referred to in 4.10.

4.3.1.3 Account should be taken of an increase of vapour pressure in harbour conditions referred to in 4.2.6.4.

4.3.1.4 The tanks should be designed for the most unfavourable static heel angle with the range 0° to 30° without exceeding allowable stresses given in 4.5.1.

4.3.2 *Internal pressure*

4.3.2.1 The internal pressure P_{eq} in bars gauge resulting from the design vapour pressure P_o and the liquid pressure P_{gd} defined in 4.3.2.2, but not including effects of liquid sloshing, should be calculated as follows:

$$P_{eq} = P_o + (P_{gd})_{max} \quad \text{(bar)}$$

Equivalent calculation procedures may be applied.

4.3.2.2 The internal liquid pressures are those created by the resulting acceleration of the centre of gravity of the cargo due to the motions of the ship referred to in 4.3.4.1. The value of internal liquid pressure P_{gd} resulting from combined effects of gravity and dynamic accelerations should be calculated as follows:

$$P_{gd} = a_\beta Z_\beta \frac{\rho}{1.02 \times 10^4} \quad \text{(bar)}$$

where:

a_β = dimensionless acceleration (i.e. relative to the acceleration of gravity), resulting from gravitational and dynamic loads, in an arbitrary direction β (see figure 4.1).

Z_β = largest liquid height (m) above the point where the pressure is to be determined, measured from the tank shell in the β direction (see figure 4.2). Tank domes considered to be part of the accepted total tank volume should be taken into account when determining Z_β unless the total volume of tank domes V_d does not exceed the following value:

$$V_d = V_t \left(\frac{100 - FL}{FL} \right)$$

where:

V_t = tank volume without any domes

FL = filling limit according to chapter 15.

ρ = maximum cargo density (kg/m³) at the design temperature.

The direction which gives the maximum value (P_{gd}) of P_{gd} should be considered. Where acceleration components in three directions need to be considered, an ellipsoid should be used instead of the ellipse in figure 4.1. The above formula applies only to full tanks.

4.3.3 External pressure

External pressure loads should be based on the difference between the minimum internal pressure (maximum vacuum) and the maximum external pressure to which any portion of the tank may be subjected simultaneously.

4.3.4 Dynamic loads due to ship motions

4.3.4.1 The determination of dynamic loads should take account of the long-term distribution of ships motions, including the effects of surge, sway, heave, roll, pitch and yaw on irregular seas which the ship will experience during its operating life (normally taken to correspond to 10^8 wave encounters). Account may be taken of reduction in dynamic loads due to necessary speed reduction and variation of heading when this consideration has also formed part of the hull strength assessment.

4.3.4.2 For design against plastic deformation and buckling the dynamic loads should be taken as the most probable largest loads the ship will encounter during its operating life (normally taken to correspond to a probability level of 10^{-8}). Guidance formulae for acceleration components are given in 4.12.

4.3.4.3 When design against fatigue is to be considered, the dynamic spectrum should be determined by long-term distribution calculation based on the operating life of the ship (normally taken to correspond to 10^8 wave encounters). If simplified dynamic loading spectra are used for the estimation of the fatigue life, those should be specially considered by the Administration.

4.3.4.4 For practical application of crack propagation estimates, simplified load distribution over a period of 15 days may be used. Such distributions may be obtained as indicated in figure 4.3.

4.3.4.5 Ships for restricted service may be given special consideration.

4.3.4.6 The accelerations acting on tanks are estimated at their centre of gravity and include the following components:

vertical acceleration:	motion accelerations of heave, pitch and, possibly, roll (normal to the ship base);
transverse acceleration:	motion accelerations of sway, yaw and roll; and gravity component of roll;
longitudinal acceleration:	motion accelerations of surge and pitch; and gravity component of pitch.

4.3.5 Sloshing loads

4.3.5.1 When partial filling is contemplated, the risk of significant loads due to sloshing induced by any of the ship motions referred to in 4.3.4.6 should be considered.

4.3.5.2 When risk of significant sloshing-induced loads is found to be present, special tests and calculations should be required.

4.3.6 Thermal loads

4.3.6.1 Transient thermal loads during cooling down periods should be considered for tanks intended for cargo temperatures below −55°C.

4.3.6.2 Stationary thermal loads should be considered for tanks where design supporting arrangement and operating temperature may give rise to significant thermal stresses.

4.3.7 Loads on supports

The loads on supports are covered by 4.6.

4.4 Structural analyses

4.4.1 Integral tanks

The structural analysis of integral tanks should be in accordance with Recognized Standards. The tank boundary scantlings should meet at least the requirements for deep tanks taking into account the internal pressure as indicated in 4.3.2, but the resulting scantlings should not be less than normally required by such standards.

4.4.2 Membrane tanks

4.4.2.1 For membrane tanks, the effects of all static and dynamic loads should be considered to determine the suitability of the membrane and of the associated insulation with respect to plastic deformation and fatigue.

4.4.2.2 Before approval is given, a model of both the primary and secondary barriers, including corners and joints, should normally be tested to verify that they will withstand the expected combined strains due to static, dynamic and thermal loads. Test conditions should represent the most extreme service conditions the cargo containment system will see in its life. Material tests should ensure that ageing is not liable to prevent the materials from carrying out their intended function.

4.4.2.3 For the purpose of the test referred to in 4.4.2.2, a complete analysis of the particular motions, accelerations and response of ships and cargo containment systems should be performed, unless these data are available from similar ships.

4.4.2.4 Special attention should be paid to the possible collapse of the membrane due to an overpressure in the interbarrier space, to a possible vacuum in the cargo tank, to the sloshing effects and to hull vibration effects.

4.4.2.5 A structural analysis of the hull should be to the satisfaction of the Administration, taking into account the internal pressure as indicated in 4.3.2. Special attention, however, should be paid to deflections of the hull and their compatibility with the membrane and associated insulation. Inner hull plating thickness should meet at least the requirements of Recognized Standards for deep tanks taking into account the internal pressure as indicated in 4.3.2. The allowable stress for the membrane, membrane-supporting material and insulation should be determined in each particular case.

4.4.3 Semi-membrane tanks

A structural analysis should be performed in accordance with the requirements for membrane tanks or independent tanks as appropriate, taking into account the internal pressure as indicated in 4.3.2.

4.4.4 Type A independent tanks

4.4.4.1 A structural analysis should be performed to the satisfaction of the Administration taking into account the internal pressure as indicated in 4.3.2. The cargo tank plating thickness should meet at least the requirements of Recognized Standards for deep tanks taking into account the internal pressure as indicated in 4.3.2 and any corrosion allowance required by 4.5.2.

4.4.4.2 For parts such as structure in way of supports not otherwise covered by Recognized Standards, stresses should be determined by direct calculations, taking into account the loads referred to in 4.3 as far as applicable, and the ship deflection in way of supports.

4.4.5 Type B independent tanks

For tanks of this type the following applies:

.1 The effects of all dynamic and static loads should be used to determine the suitability of the structure with respect to:

- plastic deformation
- buckling
- fatigue failure
- crack propagation.

Statistical wave load analysis in accordance with 4.3.4, finite element analysis or similar methods and fracture mechanics analysis or an equivalent approach, should be carried out.

.2 A three-dimensional analysis should be carried out to evaluate the stress levels contributed by the ship's hull. The model for this analysis should include the cargo tank with its supporting and keying system as well as a reasonable part of the hull.

.3 A complete analysis of the particular ship accelerations and motions in irregular waves and of the response of the ship and its cargo tanks to these forces and motions should be performed unless these data are available from similar ships.

.4 A buckling analysis should consider the maximum construction tolerances.

.5 Where deemed necessary by the Administration, model tests may be required to determine stress concentration factors and fatigue life of structural elements.

.6 The cumulative effect of the fatigue load should comply with:

$$\Sigma \frac{n_i}{N_i} + \frac{10^3}{N_j} \leqslant C_w$$

where:

$n_i \doteq$ number of stress cycles at each stress level during the life of the ship

$N_i =$ number of cycles to fracture for the respective stress level according to the Wöhler (S-N) curve

$N_j =$ number of cycles to fracture for the fatigue loads due to loading and unloading

C_w should be less than or equal to 0.5, except that the Administration may give special consideration to the use of a value greater than 0.5 but not greater than 1.0, dependent on the test procedure and data used to establish the Wöhler (S-N) curve.

4.4.6 *Type C independent tanks*

4.4.6.1 Scantlings based on internal pressure should be calculated as follows:

.1 The thickness and form of pressure-containing parts of pressure vessels under internal pressure, including flanges should be determined according to a standard acceptable to the Administration. These calculations in all cases should be based on generally accepted pressure vessel design theory. Openings in pressure-containing parts of pressure vessels should be reinforced in accordance with a standard acceptable to the Administration.

.2 The design liquid pressure defined in 4.3.2 should be taken into account in the above calculations.

.3 The welded joint efficiency factor to be used in the calculation according to 4.4.6.1.1 should be 0.95 when the inspection and the non-destructive testing referred to in 4.10.9 are carried out. This figure may be increased up to 1.0 when account is taken of other considerations, such as the material used, type of joints, welding procedure and type of loading. For process pressure vessels the Administration may accept partial non-destructive examinations, but not less than those of 4.10.9.2.2 depending on such factors as the material used, the design temperature, the nil ductility transition temperature of the material as fabricated, the type of joint and welding procedure, but in this case an efficiency factor of not more than 0.85 should be adopted. For special materials, the above-mentioned factors should be reduced depending on the specified mechanical properties of the welded joint.

4.4.6.2 Buckling criteria should be as follows:

.1 The thickness and form of pressure vessels subject to external pressure and other loads causing compressive stresses should be to a standard acceptable to the Administration. These calculations in all cases should be based on generally accepted pressure vessel buckling theory and should adequately account for the difference in theoretical and actual buckling stress as a result of plate edge misalignment, ovality and deviation from true circular form over a specified arc or chord length.

.2 The design external pressure P_e used for verifying the buckling of the pressure vessels should not be less than that given by:

$$P_e = P_1 + P_2 + P_3 + P_4 \text{ (bar)}$$

where:

P_1 = setting value of vacuum relief valves. For vessels not fitted with vacuum relief valves P_1 should be specially considered, but should not in general be taken as less than 0.25 bar.

P_2 = the set pressure of the pressure relief valves for completely closed spaces containing pressure vessels or parts of pressure vessels; elsewhere $P_2 = 0$.

P_3 = compressive actions in the shell due to the weight and contraction of insulation, weight of shell, including corrosion allowance, and other miscellaneous external pressure loads to which the pressure vessel may be subjected. These include, but are not limited to, weight of domes, weight of towers and piping, effect of product in the partially filled condition, accelerations and hull deflection. In addition, the local effect of external or internal pressure or both should be taken into account.

P_4 = external pressure due to head of water for pressure vessels or part of pressure vessels on exposed decks; elsewhere $P_4 = 0$.

4.4.6.3 Stress analysis in respect of static and dynamic loads should be performed as follows:

.1 Pressure vessel scantlings should be determined in accordance with 4.4.6.1 and .2.

.2 Calculations of the loads and stresses in way of the supports and the shell attachment of the support should be made. Loads referred to in 4.3 should be used, as applicable. Stresses in way of the supports should be to a standard acceptable to the Administration. In special cases a fatigue analysis may be required by the Administration.

.3 If required by the Administration, secondary stresses and thermal stresses should be specially considered.

4.4.6.4 For pressure vessels, the thickness calculated according to 4.4.6.1 or the thickness required by 4.4.6.2 plus the corrosion allowance, if any, should be considered as a minimum without any negative tolerance.

4.4.6.5 For pressure vessels, the minimum thickness of shell and heads including corrosion allowance, after forming, should not be less than 5 mm for carbon-manganese steels and nickel steels, 3 mm for austenitic steels or 7 mm for aluminium alloys.

4.4.7 *Internal insulation tanks*

4.4.7.1 The effects of all static and dynamic loads should be considered to determine the suitability of the tank with respect to:

- fatigue failure
- crack propagation from both free and supported surfaces
- adhesive and cohesive strength
- compressive, tensile and shear strength.

Statistical wave load analysis in accordance with 4.3.4, finite element analysis or similar methods and fracture mechanics analysis or an equivalent approach should be carried out.

4.4.7.2.1 Special attention should be given to crack resistance and to deflections of the inner hull or independent tank structure and their compatibility with the insulation materials. A three-dimensional structural analysis should be carried out to the satisfaction of the Administration. This analysis is to evaluate the stress levels and deformations contributed either by the inner hull or by the independent tank structure or both and should also take into account the internal pressure as indicated in 4.3.2. Where water ballast spaces are adjacent to the inner hull forming the supporting structure of the internal insulation tank, the analysis should take account of the dynamic loads caused by water ballast under the influence of ship motions.

4.4.7.2.2 The allowable stresses and associated deflections for the internal insulation tank and the inner hull structure or independent tank structure should be determined in each particular case.

4.4.7.2.3 Thicknesses of plating of the inner hull or of an independent tank should at least comply with the requirements of Recognized Standards, taking into account the internal pressure as indicated in 4.3.2. Tanks constructed of plane surfaces should at least comply with Recognized Standards for deep tanks.

4.4.7.3 A complete analysis of the response of ship, cargo and any ballast to accelerations and motions in irregular waves of the particular ship should be performed to the satisfaction of the Administration unless such analysis is available for a similar ship.

4.4.7.4.1 In order to confirm the design principles, prototype testing of composite models including structural elements should be carried out under combined effects of static, dynamic and thermal loads.

4.4.7.4.2 Test conditions should represent the most extreme service conditions the cargo containment system will be exposed to during the lifetime of the ship, including thermal cycles. For this purpose, 400 thermal cycles are considered to be a minimum, based upon 19 round voyages per year; where more than 19 round voyages per year are expected, a higher number of thermal cycles will be required. These 400 thermal cycles may be divided into 20 full cycles (cargo temperature to 45°C) and 380 partial cycles (cargo temperature to that temperature expected to be reached in the ballast voyage).

4.4.7.4.3 Models should be representative of the actual construction including corners, joints, pump mounts, piping penetrations and other critical areas, and should take into account variations in any material properties, workmanship and quality control.

4.4.7.4.4 Combined tension and fatigue tests should be carried out to evaluate crack behaviour of the insulation material in the case where a through crack develops in the inner hull or independent tank structure. In these tests, where applicable the crack area should be subjected to the maximum hydrostatic pressure of the ballast water.

4.4.7.5 The effects of fatigue loading should be determined in accordance with 4.4.5.6 or by an equivalent method.

4.4.7.6 For internal insulation tanks, repair procedures should be developed during the prototype testing programme for both the insulation material and the inner hull or the independent tank structure.

4.5 Allowable stresses and corrosion allowances

4.5.1 *Allowable stresses*

4.5.1.1 For integral tanks, allowable stresses should normally be those given for hull structure in Recognized Standards.

4.5.1.2 For membrane tanks, reference is made to the requirements of 4.4.2.5.

4.5.1.3 For type A independent tanks primarily constructed of plane surfaces, the stresses for primary and secondary members (stiffeners, web frames, stringers, girders) when calculated by classical analysis procedures should not exceed the lower of $R_m/2.66$ or $R_e/1.33$ for carbon-manganese steels and aluminium alloys, where R_m and R_e are defined in 4.5.1.7. However, if detailed calculations are carried out for the primary members, the equivalent stress σ_c as defined in 4.5.1.8 may be increased over that indicated above to a stress acceptable to the Administration; calculations should take into account the effects of bending, shear, axial and torsional deformation as well as the hull/cargo tank interaction forces due to the deflection of the double bottom and cargo tank bottoms.

4.5.1.4 For type B independent tanks, primarily constructed of bodies of revolution, the allowable stresses should not exceed:

$$\sigma_m \leqslant f$$
$$\sigma_L \leqslant 1.5f$$
$$\sigma_b \leqslant 1.5F$$
$$\sigma_L + \sigma_b \leqslant 1.5F$$
$$\sigma_m + \sigma_b \leqslant 1.5F$$

where:

σ_m = equivalent primary general membrane stress

σ_L = equivalent primary local membrane stress

σ_b = equivalent primary bending stress

f = the lesser of $\dfrac{R_m}{A}$ or $\dfrac{R_e}{B}$

F = the lesser of $\dfrac{R_m}{C}$ or $\dfrac{R_e}{D}$

with R_m and R_e as defined in 4.5.1.7. With regard to the stresses σ_m, σ_L and σ_b see also the definition of stress categories in 4.13. The values of A, B, C and D should be shown on the International Certificate of Fitness for the Carriage of Liquefied Gases in Bulk and should have at least the following minimum values:

	Nickel steels and carbon-manganese steels	Austenitic steels	Aluminium alloys
A	3	3.5	4
B	2	1.6	1.5
C	3	3	3
D	1.5	1.5	1.5

4.5.1.5 For type B independent tanks, primarily constructed of plane surfaces, the Administration may require compliance with additional or other stress criteria.

4.5.1.6 For type C independent tanks the maximum allowable membrane stress to be used in calculation according to 4.4.6.1.1 should be the lower of:

$$\frac{R_m}{A} \text{ or } \frac{R_e}{B}$$

where:

R_m and R_e are as defined in 4.5.1.7.

The values of A and B should be shown on the International Certificate of Fitness for the Carriage of Liquefied Gases in Bulk provided for in 1.5, and should have at least the minimum values indicated in the table of 4.5.1.4.

4.5.1.7 For the purpose of 4.5.1.3, 4.5.1.4 and 4.5.1.6 the following apply:

  .1 R_e = specified minimum yield stress at room temperature (N/mm²). If the stress-strain curve does not show a defined yield stress, the 0.2% proof stress applies.

      R_m = specified minimum tensile strength at room temperature (N/mm²).

      For welded connections in aluminium alloys the respective values of R_e or R_m in annealed conditions should be used.

  .2 The above properties should correspond to the minimum specified mechanical properties of the material, including the weld metal in the as-fabricated condition. Subject to special consideration by the Administration, account may be taken of enhanced yield stress and tensile strength at low temperature. The temperature on which the material properties are based should be shown on the International Certificate of Fitness for the Carriage of Liquefied Gases in Bulk provided for in 1.5.

4.5.1.8 The equivalent stress σ_C (von Mises, Huber) should be determined by:

$$\sigma_C = \sqrt{\sigma_x^2 + \sigma_y^2 - \sigma_x\sigma_y + 3\tau_{xy}^2}$$

where:

  σ_x = total normal stress in x-direction

  σ_y = total normal stress in y-direction

  τ_{xy} = total shear stress in x–y plane.

4.5.1.9 When the static and dynamic stresses are calculated separately and unless other methods of calculation are justified, the total stresses should be calculated according to:

$$\sigma_x = \sigma_{x.st} \pm \sqrt{\Sigma(\sigma_{x.dyn})^2}$$

$$\sigma_y = \sigma_{y.st} \pm \sqrt{\Sigma(\sigma_{y.dyn})^2}$$

$$\tau_{xy} = \tau_{xy.st} \pm \sqrt{\Sigma(\tau_{xy.dyn})^2}$$

where:

$\sigma_{x.st}, \sigma_{y.st}$ and $\tau_{xy.st}$ = static stresses

$\sigma_{x.dyn}, \sigma_{y.dyn}$ and $\tau_{xy.dyn}$ = dynamic stresses

all determined separately from acceleration components and hull strain components due to deflection and torsion.

4.5.1.10 For internal insulation tanks, reference is made to the requirement of 4.4.7.2.

4.5.1.11 Allowable stresses for materials other than those covered by chapter 6 should be subject to approval by the Administration in each case.

4.5.1.12 Stresses may be further limited by fatigue analysis, crack propagation analysis and buckling criteria.

4.5.2 Corrosion allowances

4.5.2.1 No corrosion allowance should generally be required in addition to the thickness resulting from the structural analysis. However, where there is no environmental control around the cargo tank, such as inerting, or where the cargo is of a corrosive nature, the Administration may require a suitable corrosion allowance.

4.5.2.2 For pressure vessels no corrosion allowance is generally required if the contents of the pressure vessel are non-corrosive and the external surface is protected by inert atmosphere or by an appropriate insulation with an approved vapour barrier. Paint or other thin coatings should not be credited as protection. Where special alloys are used with acceptable corrosion resistance, no corrosion allowance should be required. If the above conditions are not satisfied, the scantlings calculated according to 4.4.6 should be increased as appropriate.

4.6 Supports

4.6.1 Cargo tanks should be supported by the hull in a manner which will prevent bodily movement of the tank under static and dynamic loads while allowing contraction and expansion of the tank under temperature variations and hull deflections without due stressing of the tank and of the hull.

4.6.2 The tanks with supports should also be designed for a static angle of heel of 30° without exceeding allowable stresses given in 4.5.1.

4.6.3 The supports should be calculated for the most probable largest resulting acceleration, taking into account rotational as well as translational effects. This acceleration in a given direction may be determined as shown in figure 4.1. The half axes of the "acceleration ellipse" should be determined according to 4.3.4.2.

4.6.4 Suitable supports should be provided to withstand a collision force acting on the tank corresponding to one half the weight of the tank and cargo in the forward direction and one quarter the weight of the tank and cargo in the aft direction without deformation likely to endanger the tank structure.

4.6.5 The loads mentioned in 4.6.2 and 4.6.4 need not be combined with each other or with wave-induced loads.

4.6.6 For independent tanks and, where appropriate, for membrane and semi-membrane tanks, provision should be made to key the tanks against the rotational effects referred to in 4.6.3.

4.6.7 Antiflotation arrangements should be provided for independent tanks. The antiflotation arrangements should be suitable to withstand an upward force caused by an empty tank in a hold space flooded to the summer load draught of the ship, without plastic deformation likely to endanger the hull structure.

4.7 Secondary barrier

4.7.1 Where the cargo temperature at atmospheric pressure is below −10°C, a secondary barrier should be provided when required by 4.7.3 to act as a temporary containment for any envisaged leakage of liquid cargo through the primary barrier.

4.7.2 Where the cargo temperature at atmospheric pressure is not below −55°C, the hull structure may act as a secondary barrier. In such a case:

.1 the hull material should be suitable for the cargo temperature at atmospheric pressure as required by 4.9.2; and

.2   the design should be such that this temperature will not result in unacceptable hull stresses.

4.7.3 Secondary barriers in relation to tank types should normally be provided in accordance with the following table. For tanks which differ from the basic tank types as defined in 4.2 the secondary barrier requirements should be decided by the Administration in each case.

Cargo temperature at atmospheric pressure	−10°C and above	Below −10°C down to −55°C	Below −55°C
Basic tank type	No secondary barrier required	Hull may act as secondary barrier	Separate secondary barrier where required
Integral		Tank type not normally allowed[1]	
Membrane		Complete secondary barrier	
Semi-membrane		Complete secondary barrier[2]	
Independent			
Type A		Complete secondary barrier	
Type B		Partial secondary barrier	
Type C		No secondary barrier required	
Internal insulation			
Type 1		Complete secondary barrier	
Type 2		Complete secondary barrier is incorporated	

[1] A complete secondary barrier should normally be required if cargoes with a temperature at atmospheric pressure below −10°C are permitted in accordance with 4.2.1.3.

[2] In the case of semi-membrane tanks which comply in all respects with the requirements applicable to type B independent tanks, except for the manner of support, the Administration may, after special consideration, accept a partial secondary barrier.

4.7.4 The secondary barrier should be so designed that:

.1   it is capable of containing any envisaged leakage of liquid cargo for a period of 15 days, unless different requirements apply for particular voyages, taking into account the load spectrum referred to in 4.3.4.4;

.2   it will prevent lowering of the temperature of the ship structure to an unsafe level in the case of leakage of the primary barrier as indicated in 4.8.2; and

.3   the mechanism of failure for the primary barrier does not also cause the failure of the secondary barrier and vice versa.

4.7.5 The secondary barrier should fulfil its functions at a static angle of heel of 30°.

4.7.6.1 Where a partial secondary barrier is required, its extent should be determined on the basis of cargo leakage corresponding to the extent of failure resulting from the load spectrum referred to in 4.3.4.4 after the initial detection of a primary leak. Due account may be taken of liquid evaporation, rate of leakage, pumping capacity and other relevant factors. In all cases, however, the inner bottom adjacent to cargo tanks should be protected against liquid cargo.

4.7.6.2 Clear of the partial secondary barrier, provision such as a spray shield should be made to deflect any liquid cargo down into the space between the primary and secondary barriers and to keep the temperature of the hull structure to a safe level.

4.7.7 The secondary barrier should be capable of being periodically checked for its effectiveness, by means of a pressure/vacuum test, a visual inspection or another suitable method acceptable to the Administration. The method should be submitted to the Administration for approval.

4.8   Insulation

4.8.1 Where a product is carried at a temperature below −10°C suitable insulation should be provided to ensure that the temperature of the hull structure does not fall below the minimum allowable design temperature given in chapter 6 for the grade of steel concerned, as detailed in 4.9, when the cargo tanks are at their design temperature and the ambient temperatures are 5°C for air and 0°C for seawater. These conditions may generally be used for world-wide service. However, higher values of the ambient temperatures may be accepted by the Administration for ships operated in restricted areas. Conversely, lesser values of the ambient temperatures may be fixed by the Administration for ships trading occasionally or regularly to areas in latitudes where such lower temperatures are expected during the winter months. The ambient temperatures used in the design should be shown on the International Certificate of Fitness for the Carriage of Liquefied Gases in Bulk as provided for in 1.5.

4.8.2 Where a complete or partial secondary barrier is required, calculations should be made with the assumptions in 4.8.1 to check the temperature of the hull structure does not fall below the minimum allowable design temperature give in chapter 6 for the grade of steel concerned, as detailed in 4.9. The complete or partial secondary barrier should be assumed to be at the cargo temperature at atmospheric pressure.

4.8.3 Calculations required by 4.8.1 and 4.8.2 should be made assuming still air and still water, and except as permitted by 4.8.4, no credit should be given for means of heating. In the case referred to in 4.8.2, the cooling effect of the rising boil-off vapour from the leaked cargo should be considered in the heat transmission studies. For members connecting inner and outer hulls, the mean temperature may be taken for determining the steel grade.

4.8.4 In all cases referred to in 4.8.1 and 4.8.2 and for ambient temperature conditions of 5°C for air and 0°C for seawater, approved means of heating transverse hull structural material may be used to ensure that the temperatures of this material do not fall below the minimum allowable values. If lower àmbient temperatures are specified, approved means of heating may also be used for longitudinal hull structural material, provided this material remains suitable for the temperature conditions of 5°C for air and 0°C for seawater without heating. Such means of heating should comply with the following requirements:

.1   sufficient heat should be available to maintain the hull structure above the minimum allowable temperature in the conditions referred to in 4.8.1 and 4.8.2;

.2   the heating system should be so arranged that, in the event of a failure in any part of the system, stand-by heating could be maintained equal to not less than 100% of the theoretical heat load;

.3   the heating system should be considered as an essential auxiliary; and

.4   the design and construction of the heating system should be to the satisfaction of the Administration.

4.8.5 In determining the insulation thickness, due regard should be paid to the amount of acceptable boil-off in association with the reliquefaction plant on board, main propulsion machinery or other temperature control system.

4.9   Materials

4.9.1 The shell and deck plating of the ship and all stiffeners attached thereto should be in accordance with Recognized Standards, unless the calculated temperature of the material in the design condition is below −5°C due to the effect of the low temperature cargo, in which case the material should be in accordance with table 6.5 assuming the ambient sea and air temperature of 0°C and 5°C respectively. In the design condition, the complete or partial secondary barrier should be assumed to be at the cargo temperature at atmospheric pressure and for tanks without secondary barriers, the primary barrier should be assumed to be at the cargo temperature.

4.9.2 Hull material forming the secondary barrier should be in accordance with table 6.2. Metallic materials used in secondary barriers not forming part of the hull structure should be in accordance with table 6.2 or 6.3 as applicable. Insulation materials forming a secondary barrier should comply with the requirements of 4.9.7. Where the secondary barrier is formed by the deck or side shell plating, the material grade required by table 6.2 should be carried into the adjacent deck or side shell plating, where applicable, to a suitable extent.

4.9.3 Materials used in the construction of cargo tanks should be in accordance with table 6.1, 6.2 or 6.3.

4.9.4 Materials other than those referred to in 4.9.1, 4.9.2 and 4.9.3 used in the construction of the ship which are subject to reduced temperature due to the cargo and which do not form part of the secondary barrier should be in accordance with table 6.5 for temperatures as determined by 4.8. This includes inner bottom plating, longitudinal bulkhead plating, transverse bulkhead plating, floors, webs, stringers and all attached stiffening members.

4.9.5 The insulation materials should be suitable for loads which may be imposed on them by the adjacent structure.

4.9.6 Where applicable, due to location or environmental conditions, insulation materials should have suitable properties of resistance to fire and flame spread and should be adequately protected against penetration of water vapour and mechanical damage.

4.9.7.1 Materials used for thermal insulation should be tested for the following properties as applicable, to ensure that they are adequate for the intended service:

   .1   compatibility with the cargo

   .2   solubility in the cargo

   .3   absorption of the cargo

   .4   shrinkage

   .5   ageing

   .6   closed cell content

   .7   density

   .8   mechanical properties

   .9   thermal expansion

  .10   abrasion

  .11   cohesion

.12 thermal conductivity

.13 resistance to vibrations

.14 resistance to fire and flame spread.

4.9.7.2 In addition to meeting the above requirements, insulation materials which form part of the cargo containment as defined in 4.2.5 should be tested for the following properties after simulation of ageing and thermal cycling to ensure that they are adequate for the intended service;

.1 bonding (adhesive and cohesive strength)

.2 resistance to cargo pressure

.3 fatigue and crack propagation properties

.4 compatibility with cargo constituents and any other agent expected to be in contact with the insulation in normal service

.5 where applicable the influence of presence of water and water pressure on the insulation properties should be taken into account

.6 gas de-absorbing.

4.9.7.3 The above properties, where applicable, should be tested for the range between the expected maximum temperature in service and 5°C below the minimum design temperature, but not lower than −196°C.

4.9.8 The procedure for fabrication, storage, handling, erection, quality control and control against harmful exposure to sunlight of insulation materials should be to the satisfaction of the Administration.

4.9.9 Where powder or granulated insulation is used, the arrangements should be such as to prevent compacting of the material due to vibrations. The design should incorporate means to ensure that the material remains sufficiently buoyant to maintain the required thermal conductivity and also prevent any undue increase of pressure on the cargo containment system.

4.10 Construction and testing

4.10.1.1 All welded joints of the shells of independent tanks should be of the butt weld, full penetration type. For dome-to-shell connections, the Administration may approve tee welds of the full penetration type. Except for small penetrations on domes, nozzle welds are also generally to be designed with full penetration.

4.10.1.2 Welding joint details for type C independent tanks should be as follows:

.1 All longitudinal and circumferential joints of pressure vessels should be of butt welded, full penetration, double vee or single vee type. Full penetration butt welds should be obtained by double welding or by the use of backing rings. If used, backing rings should be removed, unless specifically approved by the Administration for very small process pressure vessels. Other edge preparations may be allowed by the Administration depending on the results of the tests carried out at the approval stage of the welding procedure.

.2 The bevel preparation of the joints between the pressure vessel body and domes and between domes and relevant fittings should be designed according to a standard for pressure vessels acceptable to the Administration. All welds connecting nozzles, domes or other penetrations of the vessel and all welds connecting flanges to the vessel or nozzles should be full penetration welds extending through the entire thickness of the vessel wall or nozzle wall, unless specially approved by the Administration for small nozzle diameters.

4.10.2 Workmanship should be to the satisfaction of the Administration. Inspection and non-destructive testing of welds for tanks other than type C independent tanks should be in accordance with the requirements of 6.3.7.

4.10.3 For membrane tanks, quality assurance measures, weld procedure qualification, design details, materials, construction, inspection and production testing of components, should be to standards developed during the prototype testing programme.

4.10.4 For semi-membrane tanks the relevant requirements in this section for independent tanks or for membrane tanks should be applied as appropriate.

4.10.5.1 For internal insulation tanks, in order to ensure uniform quality of the material, quality control procedures including environmental control, application procedure qualification, corners, penetrations and other design details, materials specification, installation and production testing of components should be to standards developed during the prototype test programme.

4.10.5.2 A quality control specification including maximum permissible size of constructional defects, tests and inspections during the fabrication, installation and also sampling tests at each of these stages should be to the satisfaction of the Administration.

4.10.6 Integral tanks should be hydrostatically or hydropneumatically tested to the satisfaction of the Administration. The test in general should be so performed that the stresses approximate, as far as practicable, to the design stresses and that the pressure at the top of the tank corresponds at least to the MARVS.

4.10.7 In ships fitted with membrane or semi-membrane tanks, cofferdams and all spaces which may normally contain liquid and are adjacent to the hull structure supporting the membrane should be hydrostatically or hydropneumatically tested in accordance with Recognized Standards. In addition, any other hold structure supporting the membrane should be tested for tightness. Pipe tunnels and other compartments which do not normally contain liquid need not be hydrostatically tested.

4.10.8.1 In ships fitted with internal insulation tanks where the inner hull is the supporting structure, all inner hull structure should be hydrostatically or hydropneumatically tested in accordance with Recognized Standards, taking into account the MARVS.

4.10.8.2 In ships fitted with internal insulation tanks where independent tanks are the supporting structure, the independent tanks should be tested in accordance with 4.10.10.1.

4.10.8.3 For internal insulation tanks where the inner hull structure or an independent tank structure acts as a secondary barrier, a tightness test of those structures should be carried out using techniques to the satisfaction of the Administration.

4.10.8.4 These tests should be performed before the application of the materials which will form the internal insulation tank.

4.10.9 For type C independent tanks, inspection and non-destructive testing should be as follows:

> **.1** *Manufacture and workmanship* — The tolerances relating to manufacture and workmanship such as out-of-roundness, local deviations from the true form, welded joints alignment and tapering of plates having different thicknesses, should comply with standards acceptable to the Administration. The tolerances should all be related to the buckling analysis referred to in 4.4.6.2.

> **.2** *Non-destructive testing* — As far as completion and extension of non-destructive testing of welded joints are concerned, the extent of non-destructive testing should be total or partial according to standards acceptable to the Administration, but the controls to be carried out should not be less than the following:

> **.2.1** Total non-destructive testing referred to in 4.4.6.1.3:
>
> Radiography:
>> butt welds 100% and
>
> Surface crack detection:
>> all welds 10%;
>>
>> reinforcement rings around holes, nozzles, etc. 100%.
>
> As an alternative, ultrasonic testing may be accepted as a partial substitute for the radiographic testing, if specially allowed by the

Administration. In addition, the Administration may require total ultrasonic testing on welding of reinforcement rings around holes, nozzles, etc.

.2.2 Partial non-destructive testing referred to in 4.4.6.1.3:

Radiography:

butt welds: all welded crossing joints and at least 10% of the full length at selected positions uniformly distributed and

Surface crack detection:

reinforcement rings around holes, nozzles, etc., 100%

Ultrasonic testing:

as may be required by the Administration in each instance.

4.10.10 Each independent tank should be subjected to a hydrostatic or hydropneumatic test as follows:

.1 For type A independent tanks, this test should be so performed that the stresses approximate, as far as practicable, to the design stresses and that the pressure at the top of the tank corresponds at least to the MARVS. When a hydropneumatic test is performed, the conditions should simulate, as far as practicable, the actual loading of the tank and of its supports.

.2 For type B independent tanks, the test should be performed as required in 4.10.10.1 for type A independent tanks. In addition, the maximum primary membrane stress or maximum bending stress in primary members under test conditions should not exceed 90% of the yield strength of the material (as fabricated) at the test temperature. To ensure that this condition is satisfied, when calculations indicate that this stress exceeds 75% of the yield strength, the prototype test should be monitored by the use of strain gauges or other suitable equipment.

.3 Type C independent tanks should be tested as follows:

.3.1 Each pressure vessel, when completely manufactured, should be subjected to a hydrostatic test at a pressure measured at the top of the tanks, of not less than $1.5P_o$, but in no case during the pressure test should the calculated primary membrane stress at any point exceed 90% of the yield stress of the material. The definition of P_o is given in 4.2.6. To ensure that this condition is satisfied where calculations indicate that this stress will exceed 0.75 times the yield strength, the prototype test should be monitored by the use of strain gauges or other suitable equipment in pressure vessels other than simple cylindrical and spherical pressure vessels.

.3.2 The temperature of the water used for the test should be at least 30°C above the nil ductility transition temperature of the material as fabricated.

.3.3 The pressure should be held for 2 h per 25 mm of thickness but in no case less than 2 h.

.3.4 Where necessary for cargo pressure vessels, and with the specific approval of the Administration, a hydropneumatic test may be carried out under the conditions prescribed in 4.10.10.3.1, .2 and .3.

.3.5 Special consideration may be given by the Administration to the testing of tanks in which higher allowable stresses are used, depending on service temperature. However, the requirements of 4.10.10.3.1 should be fully complied with.

.3.6 After completion and assembly, each pressure vessel and its related fittings should be subjected to an adequate tightness test.

.3.7 Pneumatic testing of pressure vessels other than cargo tanks should be considered on an individual case basis by the Administration. Such testing should be permitted only for those vessels which are so designed or supported that they cannot be safely filled with water, or for those vessels which cannot be dried and are to be used in a service where traces of the testing medium cannot be tolerated.

4.10.11 All tanks should be subjected to a tightness test which may be performed in combination with the pressure test referred to in 4.10.10 or separately.

4.10.12 Requirements with respect to inspection of secondary barriers should be decided by the Administration in each case.

4.10.13 In ships fitted with type B independent tanks, at least one tank and its support should be instrumented to confirm stress levels unless the design and arrangement for the size of ship involved are supported by full-scale experience. Similar instrumentation may be required by the Administration for type C independent tanks dependent on their configuration and on the arrangement of their supports and attachments.

4.10.14 The overall performance of the cargo containment system should be verified for compliance with the design parameters during the initial cool-down, loading and discharging of the cargo. Records of the performance of the components and equipment essential to verify the design parameters should be maintained and be available to the Administration.

4.10.15 Heating arrangements, if fitted in accordance with 4.8.4, should be tested for required heat output and heat distribution.

4.10.16 The hull should be inspected for cold spots following the first loaded voyage.

4.10.17 The insulation materials of internal insulation tanks should be subjected to additional inspection in order to verify their surface conditions after the third loaded voyage of the ship, but not later than the first six months of the ship's service after building or a major repair work is undertaken on the internal insulation tanks.

4.10.18 For type C independent tanks, the required marking of the pressure vessel should be achieved by a method which does not cause unacceptable local stress raisers.

4.11 Stress relieving for type C independent tanks

4.11.1 For type C independent tanks of carbon and carbon-manganese steel, post-weld heat treatment should be performed after welding if the design temperature is below −10°C. Post-weld heat treatment in all other cases and for materials other than those mentioned above should be to the satisfaction of the Administration. The soaking temperature and holding time should be to the satisfaction of the Administration.

4.11.2 In the case of large cargo pressure vessels of carbon or carbon-manganese steel for which it is difficult to perform the heat treatment, mechanical stress relieving by pressurizing may be carried out as an alternative to the heat treatment with the approval of the Administration and subject to the following conditions:

  .1 Complicated welded pressure vessel parts, such as sumps or domes with nozzles, with adjacent shell plates should be heat treated before they are welded to larger parts of the pressure vessel.

  .2 The mechanical stress relieving process should preferably be carried out during the hydrostatic pressure test required by paragraph 4.10.10.3 by applying a higher pressure than the test pressure required by 4.10.10.3.1. The pressurizing medium should be water.

  .3 For the water temperature, paragraph 4.10.10.3.2 applies.

  .4 Stress relieving should be performed while the tank is supported by its regular saddles or supporting structure or, when stress relieving cannot be carried out on board, in a manner which will give the same stresses and stress distribution as when supported by its regular saddles or supporting structure.

  .5 The maximum stress relieving pressure should be held for 2 h per 25 mm of thickness but in no case less than 2 h.

  .6 The upper limits placed on the calculated stress levels during stress relieving should be the following:

     − equivalent general primary membrane stress: $0.9R_e$

- equivalent stress composed of primary
   bending stress plus membrane stress: $1.35R_e$

where R_e is the specific lower minimum yield stress or 0.2% proof stress at test temperature of the steel used for the tank.

.7 Strain measurements will normally be required to prove these limits for at least the first tank of a series of identical tanks built consecutively. The location of strain gauges should be included in the mechanical stress relieving procedure to be submitted in accordance with 4.11.2.14.

.8 The test procedure should demonstrate that a linear relationship between pressure and strain is achieved at the end of the stress relieving process when the pressure is raised again up to the design pressure.

.9 High stress areas in way of geometrical discontinuities such as nozzles and other openings should be checked for cracks by dye penetrant or magnetic particle inspection after mechanical stress relieving. Particular attention in this respect should be given to plates exceeding 30 mm in thickness.

.10 Steels which have a ratio of yield stress to ultimate tensile strength greater than 0.8 should generally not be mechanically stress relieved. If, however, the yield stress is raised by a method giving high ductility of the steel, slightly higher rates may be accepted upon consideration in each case.

.11 Mechanical stress relieving cannot be substituted for heat treatment of cold-formed parts of tanks if the degree of cold forming exceeds the limit above which heat treatment is required.

.12 The thickness of the shell and heads of the tank should not exceed 40 mm. Higher thicknesses may be accepted for parts which are thermally stress relieved.

.13 Local buckling should be guarded against particularly when torispherical heads are used for tanks and domes.

.14 The procedure for mechanical stress relieving should be submitted beforehand to the Administration for approval.

4.12 Guidance formulae for acceleration components

The following formulae are given as guidance for the components of acceleration due to ship's motions corresponding to a probability level of 10^{-8} in the North Atlantic and apply to ships with a length exceeding 50 m.

Vertical acceleration as defined in 4.3.4.6

$$a_z = \pm a_o \sqrt{1 + \left(5.3 - \frac{45}{L_o}\right)^2 \left(\frac{x}{L_o} + 0.05\right)^2 \left(\frac{0.6}{C_B}\right)^{1.5}}$$

Transverse acceleration as defined in 4.3.4.6

$$a_y = \pm a_o \sqrt{0.6 + 2.5\left(\frac{x}{L_o} + 0.05\right)^2 + K\left(1 + 0.6K\frac{z}{B}\right)^2}$$

Longitudinal acceleration as defined in 4.3.4.6

$$a_x = \pm a_o \sqrt{0.06 + A^2 - 0.25A}$$

with:

$$A = \left(0.7 - \frac{L_o}{1200} + 5\frac{z}{L_o}\right)\left(\frac{0.6}{C_B}\right)$$

where:

L_o = length of the ship for determination of scantlings as defined in Recognized Standards (m)

C_B = block coefficient

B = greatest moulded breadth of the ship (m)

x = longitudinal distance (m) from amidships to the centre of gravity of the tank with contents; x is positive forward of amidships, negative aft of amidships

z = vertical distance (m) from the ship's actual waterline to the centre of gravity of the tank with contents; z is positive above and negative below the waterline

a_o $= 0.2\dfrac{V}{\sqrt{L_o}} + \dfrac{34 - \dfrac{600}{L_o}}{L_o}$

     where V = service speed (knots)

K = 1 in general. For particular loading conditions and hull forms, determination of K according to the formula below may be necessary

     $K = \dfrac{13GM}{B}$ where $K \geqslant 1.0$ and GM = metacentric height (m).

a_x, a_y and a_z = maximum dimensionless accelerations (i.e. relative to the acceleration of gravity) in the respective directions, and they are considered as acting separately for calculation purposes;

a_z does not include the component due to the static weight, a_y includes the component due to the static weight in the transverse direction due to rolling and a_x includes the component due to the static weight in the longitudinal direction due to pitching.

4.13 Stress categories

For the purpose of stress evaluation referred to in 4.5.1.4, stress categories are defined in this section.

4.13.1 Normal stress is the component of stress normal to the plane of reference.

4.13.2 Membrane stress is the component of normal stress which is uniformly distributed and equal to the average value of the stress across the thickness of the section under consideration.

4.13.3 Bending stress is the variable stress across the thickness of the section under consideration, after the subtraction of the membrane stress.

4.13.4 Shear stress is the component of the stress acting in the plane of reference.

4.13.5 Primary stress is a stress produced by the imposed loading and which is necessary to balance the external forces and moments. The basic characteristic of a primary stress is that it is not self-limiting. Primary stresses which considerably exceed the yield strength will result in failure or at least in gross deformations.

4.13.6 Primary general membrane stress is a primary membrane stress which is so distributed in the structure that no redistribution of load occurs as a result of yielding.

4.13.7 Primary local membrane stress arises where a membrane stress produced by pressure or other mechanical loading and associated with a primary or a discontinuity effect produces excessive distortion in the transfer of loads for other portions of the structure. Such a stress is classified as a primary local membrane stress although it has some characteristics of a secondary stress. A stress region may be considered as local if:

$$S_1 \leqslant 0.5 \sqrt{Rt} \text{ and}$$
$$S_2 \geqslant 2.5 \sqrt{Rt}$$

where:

S_1 = distance in the meridional direction over which the equivalent stress exceeds 1.1f

S_2 = distance in the meridional direction to another region where the limits for primary general membrane stress are exceeded

R = mean radius of the vessel

t = wall thickness of the vessel at the location where the primary general membrane stress limit is exceeded

f = allowable primary general membrane stress.

4.13.8 Secondary stress is a normal stress or shear stress developed by constraints of adjacent parts or by self-constraint of a structure. The basic characteristic of a secondary stress is that it is self-limiting. Local yielding and minor distortions can satisfy the conditions which cause the stress to occur.

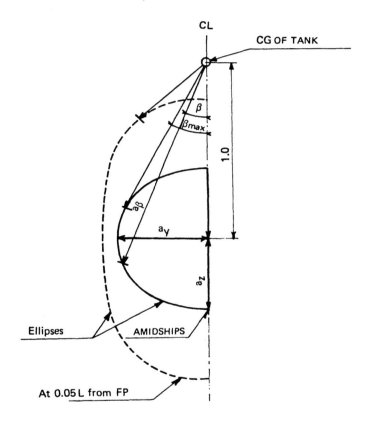

a_β = resulting acceleration (static and dynamic) in arbitrary direction β

a_y = transverse component of acceleration

a_z = vertical component of acceleration

Figure 4.1 – *Acceleration ellipse*

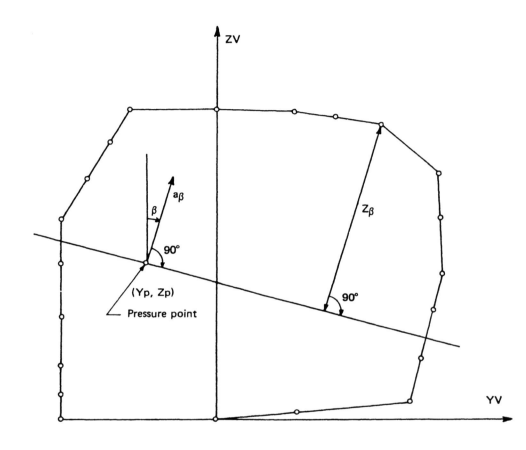

Figure 4.2 – *Determination of internal pressure heads*

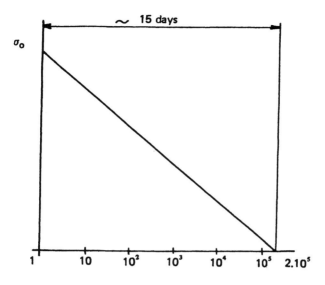

Response cycles

σ_o = most probable maximum stress over the life of the ship

Response cycle scale is logarithmic; the value of 2.10^5 is given as an example of estimate.

Figure 4.3 – *Simplified load distribution*

Chapter 5

Process pressure vessels and liquid, vapour, and pressure piping systems

5.1 General

5.1.1 Administrations should take appropriate steps to ensure uniformity in the implementation and application of the provisions of this chapter.*

5.1.2 The requirements for type C independent tanks in chapter 4 may also apply to process pressure vessels if required by the Administration. If so required the term "pressure vessels" as used in chapter 4 covers both type C independent tanks and process pressure vessels.

5.2 Cargo and process piping

5.2.1 General

5.2.1.1 The requirements of sections 5.2 to 5.5 apply to product and process piping including vapour piping and vent lines of safety valves or similar piping. Instrument piping not containing cargo is exempt from these requirements.

5.2.1.2 Provision should be made by the use of offsets, loops, bends, mechanical expansion joints such as bellows, slip joints and ball joints or similar suitable means to protect the piping, piping system components and cargo tanks from excessive stresses due to thermal movement and from movements of the tank and hull structure. Where mechanical expansion joints are used in piping they should be held to a minimum and, where located outside cargo tanks, should be of the bellows type.

5.2.1.3 Low-temperature piping should be thermally isolated from the adjacent hull structure, where necessary, to prevent the temperature of the hull from falling below the design temperature of the hull material. Where liquid piping is dismantled regularly, or where liquid leakage may be anticipated, such as at shore connections and at pump seals, protection for the hull beneath should be provided.

---

* Refer to the published Rules of members and associate members of the International Association of Classification Societies and in particular *IACS Unified Requirement No. G3.*

5.2.1.4 Where tanks or piping are separated from the ship's structure by thermal isolation, provision should be made for electrically bonding both the piping and the tanks. All gasketed pipe joints and hose connections should be electrically bonded.

5.2.1.5 Suitable means should be provided to relieve the pressure and remove liquid contents from cargo loading and discharging crossover headers and cargo hoses to the cargo tanks or other suitable location, prior to disconnecting the cargo hoses.

5.2.1.6 All pipelines or components which may be isolated in a liquid-full condition should be provided with relief valves.

5.2.1.7 Relief valves discharging liquid cargo from the cargo piping system should discharge into the cargo tanks; alternatively they may discharge to the cargo vent mast if means are provided to detect and dispose of any liquid cargo which may flow into the vent system. Relief valves on cargo pumps should discharge to the pump suction.

5.2.2 Scantlings based on internal pressure

5.2.2.1 Subject to the conditions stated in 5.2.4, the wall thickness of pipes should not be less than:

$$t = \frac{t_o + b + c}{1 - \dfrac{a}{100}} \quad \text{(mm)}$$

where:

t_o = theoretical thickness

t_o = $PD/(20Ke + P)$ (mm)

    with:

    P = design pressure (bar) referred to in 5.2.3

    D = outside diameter (mm)

    K = allowable stress (N/mm²) referred to in 5.2.4

    e = efficiency factor equal to 1.0 for seamless pipes and for longitudinally or spirally welded pipes, delivered by approved manufacturers of welded pipes, which are considered equivalent to seamless pipes when non-destructive testing on welds is carried out in accordance with Recognized Standards. In other cases an efficiency factor value depending on the manufacturing process may be determined by the Administration.

b = allowance for bending (mm). The value of b should be chosen so that the calculated stress in the bend, due to internal pressure only, does not exceed the allowable stress. Where such justification is not given, b should be:

$$b = \frac{Dt_o}{2.5r} \quad (mm)$$

with:

r = mean radius of the bend (mm)

c = corrosion allowance (mm). If corrosion or erosion is expected, the wall thickness of the piping should be increased over that required by other design requirements. This allowance should be consistent with the expected life of the piping.

a = negative manufacturing tolerance for thickness (%)

5.2.3 Design pressure

5.2.3.1 The design pressure P in the formula for t_o in 5.2.2.1 is the maximum gauge pressure to which the system may be subjected in service.

5.2.3.2 The greater of the following design conditions should be used for piping, piping systems and components as appropriate:

.1 for vapour piping systems or components which may be separated from their relief valves and which may contain some liquid: the saturated vapour pressure at 45°C, or higher or lower if agreed upon by the Administration (see 4.2.6.2);

.2 for systems or components which may be separated from their relief valves and which contain only vapour at all times: the superheated vapour pressure at 45°C or higher or lower if agreed upon by the Administration (see 4.2.6.2), assuming an initial condition of saturated vapour in the system at the system operating pressure and temperature; or

.3 the MARVS of the cargo tanks and cargo processing systems; or

.4 the pressure setting of the associated pump or compressor discharge relief valve; or

.5 the maximum total discharge or loading head of the cargo piping system; or

.6 the relief valve setting on a pipeline system.

5.2.3.3 The design pressure should not be less than 10 bar gauge except for open-ended lines where it should be not less than 5 bar gauge.

5.2.4 *Permissible stresses*

5.2.4.1 For pipes, the permissible stress to be considered in the formula for t in 5.2.2.1 is the lower of the following values:

$$\frac{R_m}{A} \text{ or } \frac{R_e}{B}$$

where:

R_m = specified minimum tensile strength at room temperature (N/mm^2)

R_e = specified minimum yield stress at room temperature (N/mm^2). If the stress–strain curve does not show a defined yield stress, the 0.2% proof stress applies.

The values of A and B should be shown on the International Certificate of Fitness for the Carriage of Liquefied Gases in Bulk as provided for in 1.5 and have values of at least $A = 2.7$ and $B = 1.8$.

5.2.4.2 The minimum wall thickness should be in accordance with Recognized Standards.

5.2.4.3 Where necessary for mechanical strength to prevent damage, collapse, excessive sag or buckling of pipes due to superimposed loads from supports, ship deflection or other causes, the wall thickness should be increased over that required by 5.2.2, or, if this is impracticable or would cause excessive local stresses, these loads should be reduced, protected against or eliminated by other design methods.

5.2.4.4 Flanges, valves and other fittings should be to a standard acceptable to the Administration, taking into account the design pressure defined in 5.2.2. For bellows expansion joints used in vapour service, a lower minimum design pressure may be accepted by the Administration.

5.2.4.5 For flanges not complying with a standard, the dimensions of flanges and related bolts should be to the satisfaction of the Administration.

5.2.5 *Stress analysis*

When the design temperature is −110°C or lower, a complete stress analysis, taking into account all the stresses due to weight of pipes, including acceleration loads if significant, internal pressure, thermal contraction and loads induced by hog and sag of the ship for each branch of the piping system should be submitted to the Administration. For temperatures of above −110°C, a stress analysis may be required by the Administration in relation to such matters as the design or stiffness of the piping system and the choice of materials. In any case, consideration should be given to thermal stresses, even though calculations are not submitted. The analysis may be carried out according to a code of practice acceptable to the Administration.

5.2.6 *Materials*

5.2.6.1 The choice and testing of materials used in piping systems should comply with the requirements of chapter 6 taking into account the minimum design temperature. However, some relaxation may be permitted in the quality of material of open-ended vent piping, provided the temperature of the cargo at the pressure relief valve setting is −55°C or greater and provided no liquid discharge to the vent piping can occur. Similar relaxations may be permitted under the same temperature conditions to open-ended piping inside cargo tanks, excluding discharge piping and all piping inside membrane and semi-membrane tanks.

5.2.6.2 Materials having a melting point below 925°C should not be used for piping outside the cargo tanks except for short lengths of pipes attached to the cargo tanks, in which case fire-resisting insulation should be provided.

5.3 Type tests on piping components

5.3.1 Each type of piping component should be subject to type tests.

5.3.2.1 Each size and type of valve intended to be used at a working temperature below −55°C should be subjected to a tightness test to the minimum design temperature or lower, and to a pressure not lower than the design pressure of the valve. During the test, satisfactory operation of the valve should be ascertained.

5.3.2.2 The following type tests should be performed on each type of expansion bellows intended for use on cargo piping outside the cargo tank and, where required, on those expansion bellows installed within the cargo tanks:

   .1   A type element of the bellows, not precompressed, should be pressure tested at not less than five times the design pressure without bursting. The duration of the test should not be less than five minutes.

   .2   A pressure test should be performed on a type expansion joint complete with all the accessories such as flanges, stays and articulations, at twice the design pressure at the extreme displacement conditions recommended by the manufacturer without permanent deformation. Depending on the materials used, the Administration may require the test to be at the minimum design temperature.

   .3   A cyclic test (thermal movements) should be performed on a complete expansion joint, which is to successfully withstand at least as many cycles, under the conditions of pressure, temperature, axial movement, rotational movement and transverse movement, as it will encounter in actual service. Testing at ambient temperature is permitted, when this testing is at least as severe as testing at the service temperature.

.4 A cyclic fatigue test (ship deformation) should be performed on a complete expansion joint, without internal pressure, by simulating the bellows movement corresponding to a compensated pipe length, for at least 2,000,000 cycles at a frequency not higher than 5 cycles/s. This test is only required when, due to the piping arrangement, ship deformation loads are actually experienced.

.5 The Administration may waive performance of the tests referred to in this paragraph provided that complete documentation is supplied to establish the suitability of the expansion joints to withstand the expected working conditions. When the maximum internal pressure exceeds 1.0 bar gauge this documentation is to include sufficient test data to justify the design method used, with particular reference to correlation between calculation and test results.

5.4 Piping fabrication and joining details

5.4.1 The requirements of this section apply to piping inside and outside the cargo tanks. However, the Administration may accept relaxations from these requirements for piping inside cargo tanks and open-ended piping.

5.4.2 The following direct connection of pipe lengths, without flanges, may be considered:

.1 Butt-welded joints with complete penetration at the root may be used in all applications. For design temperatures below −10°C, butt welds should be either double welded or equivalent to a double welded butt joint. This may be accomplished by use of a backing ring, consumable insert or inert gas back-up on the first pass. For design pressures in excess of 10 bar and design temperatures of −10°C or lower, backing rings should be removed.

.2 Slip-on welded joints with sleeves and related welding, having dimensions satisfactory to the Administration, should only be used for open-ended lines with external diameter of 50 mm or less and design temperatures not lower than −55°C.

.3 Screwed couplings acceptable to the Administration should only be used for accessory lines and instrumentation lines with external diameters of 25 mm or less.

5.4.3.1 Flanges in flange connections should be of the welded neck, slip-on or socket welded type.

5.4.3.2 Flanges should comply with standards acceptable to the Administration as to their type, manufacture and test. In particular, for all piping except open ended, the following restrictions apply:

69

.1 For design temperatures lower than −55°C, only welded neck flanges should be used.

.2 For design temperatures lower than −10°C, slip-on flanges should not be used in nominal sizes above 100 mm and socket welded flanges should not be used in nominal sizes above 50 mm.

5.4.4 Piping connections, other than those mentioned in 5.4.2 and .3, may be accepted by the Administration in each case.

5.4.5 Bellows and expansion joints should be provided to allow for expansion of piping.

.1 If necessary, bellows should be protected against icing.

.2 Slip joints should not be used except within the cargo tanks.

5.4.6 *Welding, post-weld heat treatment and non-destructive testing*

.1 Welding should be carried out in accordance with 6.3.

.2 Post-weld heat treatment should be required for all butt welds of pipes made with carbon, carbon-manganese and low alloy steels. The Administration may waive the requirement for thermal stress relieving of pipes having wall thickness less than 10 mm in relation to the design temperature and pressure of the piping system concerned.

.3 In addition to normal controls before and during the welding and to the visual inspection of the finished welds, as necessary for proving that the welding has been carried out correctly and according to the requirements of this paragraph, the following tests should be required:

.3.1 100% radiographic inspection of butt-welded joints for piping systems with design temperatures lower than −10°C and with inside diameters of more than 75 mm or wall thicknesses greater than 10 mm. When such butt-welded joints of piping sections are made by automatic welding procedures in the pipe fabrication shop, upon special approval by the Administration, the extent of radiographic inspection may be progressively reduced but in no case to less than 10% of each joint. If defects are revealed the extent of examination should be increased to 100% and should include inspection of previously accepted welds. This special approval can only be granted if well-documented quality assurance procedures and records are available to enable the Administration to assess the ability of the manufacturer to produce satisfactory welds consistently.

.3.2 For other butt-welded joints of pipes not covered by 5.4.6.3.1, spot radiographic tests or other non-destructive tests should be carried out at the discretion of the Administration depending upon service, position and materials. In general, at least 10% of butt-welded joints of pipes should be radiographed.

5.5   Testing of piping

5.5.1 The requirements of this section apply to piping inside and outside the cargo tanks. However, the Administration may accept relaxations from these requirements for piping inside cargo tanks and open-ended piping.

5.5.2 After assembly, all cargo and process piping should be subjected to a hydrostatic test to at least 1.5 times the design pressure. When piping systems or parts of systems are completely manufactured and equipped with all fittings, the hydrostatic test may be conducted prior to installation aboard ship. Joints welded on board should be hydrostatically tested to at least 1.5 times the design pressure. Where water cannot be tolerated and the piping cannot be dried prior to putting the system into service, proposals for alternative testing fluids or testing means should be submitted to the Administration for approval.

5.5.3 After assembly on board, each cargo and process piping system should be subjected to a leak test using air, halides, or other suitable medium to a pressure depending on the leak detection method applied.

5.5.4 All piping systems including valves, fittings and associated equipment for handling cargo or vapours should be tested under normal operating conditions not later than at the first loading operation.

5.6   Cargo system valving requirements

5.6.1 Every cargo piping system and cargo tank should be provided with the following valves, as applicable:

.1   For cargo tanks with a MARVS not exceeding 0.7 bar gauge, all liquid and vapour connections, except safety relief valves and liquid level gauging devices, should have shutoff valves located as close to the tank as practicable. These valves may be remotely controlled but should be capable of local manual operation and provide full closure. One or more remotely controlled emergency shutdown valves should be provided on the ship for shutting down liquid and vapour cargo transfer between ship and shore. Such valves may be arranged to suit the ship's design and may be the same valve as required in 5.6.3 and should comply with the requirements of 5.6.4.

.2   For cargo tanks with a MARVS exceeding 0.7 bar gauge, all liquid and vapour connections, except safety relief valves and liquid level gauging devices, should be equipped with a manually operated stop valve and a remotely controlled emergency shutdown valve. These valves should be located as close to the tank as practicable. Where the pipe size does not exceed 50 mm in diameter, excess flow valves may be used in lieu of the emergency shutdown valve. A single valve may be substituted for the two separate valves provided the valve complies with the requirements of 5.6.4, is capable of local manual operation and provides full closure of the line.

.3 Cargo pumps and compressors should be arranged to shutdown automatically if the emergency shutdown valves required by 5.6.1.1 and .2 are closed by the emergency shutdown system required by 5.6.4.

5.6.2 Cargo tank connections for gauging or measuring devices need not be equipped with excess flow or emergency shutdown valves provided that the devices are so constructed that the outward flow of tank contents cannot exceed that passed by a 1.5 mm diameter circular hole.

5.6.3 One remotely operated emergency shutdown valve should be provided at each cargo hose connection in use. Connections not used in transfer operations may be blinded with blank flanges in lieu of valves.

5.6.4 The control system for all required emergency shutdown valves should be so arranged that all such valves may be operated by single controls situated in at least two remote locations on the ship. One of these locations should be the control position required by 13.1.3 or cargo control room. The control system should also be provided with fusible elements designed to melt at temperatures between 98°C and 104°C which will cause the emergency shutdown valves to close in the event of fire. Locations for such fusible elements should include the tank domes and loading stations. Emergency shutdown valves should be of the fail-closed (closed on loss of power) type and be capable of local manual closing operation. Emergency shutdown valves in liquid piping should fully close under all service conditions with 30 s of actuation. Information about the closing time of the valves and their operating characteristics should be available on board and the closing time should be verifiable and reproducible. Such valves should close smoothly.

5.6.5 Excess flow valves should close automatically at the rated closing flow of vapour or liquid as specified by the manufacturer. The piping including fittings, valves, and appurtenances protected by an excess flow valve, should have a greater capacity than the rated closing flow of the excess flow valve. Excess flow valves may be designed with a bypass not exceeding an area of 1.0 mm diameter circular opening to allow equalization of pressure, after an operating shutdown.

5.7 Ship's cargo hoses

5.7.1 Liquid and vapour hoses used for cargo transfer should be compatible with the cargo and suitable for the cargo temperature.

5.7.2 Hoses subject to tank pressure, or the discharge pressure of pumps or vapour compressors, should be designed for a bursting pressure not less than five times the maximum pressure the hose will be subjected to during cargo transfer.

5.7.3 Each new type of cargo hose, complete with end fittings, should be prototype tested to a pressure not less than five times its specified maximum working pressure. The hose temperature during this prototype test should be the intended extreme service temperature. Hoses used for prototype testing should not be used for cargo service. Thereafter, before being placed in service, each new length of cargo hose produced should be hydrostatically tested at ambient temperature to a pressure not less than 1.5 times its specified maximum working pressure nor more than two fifths its bursting pressure. The hose should be stencilled or otherwise marked with its specified maximum working pressure and, if used in other than ambient temperature services, its maximum or minimum service temperature or both. The specified maximum working pressure should not be less than 10 bar gauge.

5.8   Cargo transfer methods

5.8.1   Where cargo transfer is by means of cargo pumps not accessible for repair with the tanks in service, at least two separate means should be provided to transfer cargo from each cargo tank and the design should be such that failure of one cargo pump, or means of transfer, will not prevent the cargo transfer by another pump or pumps, or other cargo transfer means.

5.8.2 The procedure for transfer of cargo by gas pressurization should preclude lifting of the relief valves during such transfer. Gas pressurization may be accepted as a means of transfer of cargo for those tanks so designed that the design factor of safety is not reduced under the conditions prevailing during the cargo transfer operation.

5.9   Vapour return connections

Connections for vapour return lines to the shore installations should be provided.

Chapter 6

Materials of construction

6.1 General

6.1.1 Administrations should take appropriate steps to ensure uniformity in the implementation and application of the provisions of this chapter.*

6.1.2 This chapter gives the requirements for plates, sections, pipes, forgings, castings and weldments used in the construction of cargo tanks, cargo process pressure vessels, cargo and process piping, secondary barriers and contiguous hull structures associated with the transportation of the products. The requirements for rolled materials, forgings and castings are given in 6.2 and tables 6.1 to 6.5. The requirements for weldments are given in 6.3.

6.1.3 The manufacture, testing, inspection and documentation should be in accordance with Recognized Standards and the specific requirements given in this Code.

6.1.4.1 Acceptance tests should include Charpy V-notch toughness tests unless otherwise specified by the Administration. The specified Charpy V-notch requirements are minimum average energy values for three full-size (10 mm × 10 mm) specimens and minimum single energy values for individual specimens. Dimensions and tolerances of Charpy V-notch specimens should be in accordance with Recognized Standards. The testing and requirements for specimens smaller than 5.0 mm size should be in accordance with Recognized Standards. Minimum average values for subsized specimens should be:

Charpy V-notch specimen size (mm)	Minimum energy average of three specimens
10 × 10	*E*
10 × 7.5	5/6 *E*
10 x 5.0	2/3 *E*

where: E = the energy values (J) specified in tables 6.1 to 6.4.

---

* Refer to the published Rules of members and associate members of the International Association of Classification Societies and in particular to *IACS Unified Requirement No. W1.*

Single-V butt weld

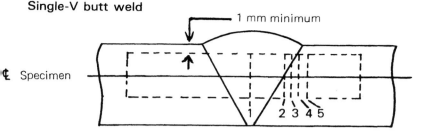

℄ Specimen

Double-V butt weld

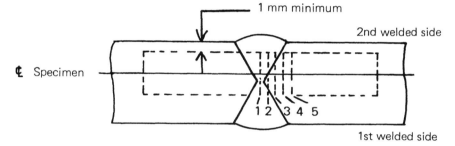

℄ Specimen

Notch location:

1   Centre of weld
2   On fusion line
3   In heat-affected zone (HAZ), 1 mm from fusion line
4   In HAZ, 3 mm from fusion line
5   In HAZ, 5 mm from fusion line

The largest-size Charpy specimens possible for the material thickness should be machined with the centre of the specimens located as near as practicable to a point midway between the surface and the centre of the thickness. In all cases, the distance from the surface of the material to the edge of the specimen should be approximately 1 mm or greater. In addition, for double-V butt welds, specimens should be machined closer to the surface of the second welded section.

Figure 6.1 – *Orientation of weld test specimen*

Only one individual value may be below the specified average value provided it is not less than 70% of that value.

6.1.4.2 In all cases, the largest-size Charpy specimens possible for the material thickness should be machined with the specimens located as near as practicable to a point midway between the surface and the centre of the thickness and the length of the notch perpendicular to the surface (see figure 6.1). If the average value of the three initial Charpy V-notch specimens fails to meet the stated requirements, or the value for more than one specimen is below the required average value, or when the value for one specimen is below the minimum value permitted for a single specimen, three additional specimens from the same material may be tested and the results combined with those previously obtained to form a new average. If this new average complies with the requirements and if no more than two individual results are lower than the required average and no more than one result is lower than the required value for a single specimen, the piece or batch may be accepted. At the discretion of the Administration other types of toughness tests, such as a drop weight test, may be used. This may be in addition to or in lieu of the Charpy V-notch test.

6.1.5 Tensile strength, yield stress and elongation should be to the satisfaction of the Administration. For carbon-manganese steel and other materials with definitive yield points, consideration should be given to the limitation of the yield to tensile ratio.

6.1.6 The bend test may be omitted as a material acceptance test, but is required for weld tests.

6.1.7 Materials with alternative chemical composition or mechanical properties may be accepted by the Administration.

6.1.8 Where post-weld heat treatment is specified or required, the properties of the base material should be determined in the heat treated condition in accordance with the applicable table of this chapter and the weld properties should be determined in the heat treated condition in accordance with 6.3. In cases where a post-weld heat treatment is applied, the test requirements may be modified at the discretion of the Administration.

6.1.9 Where reference is made in this chapter to A, B, D, E, AH, DH and EH hull structural steels, these steel grades are hull structural steels according to Recognized Standards.

6.2 Material requirements

The requirements for materials of construction are shown in the tables as follows:

Table 6.1: Plates, pipes (seamless and welded), sections and forgings for cargo tanks and process pressure vessels for design temperatures not lower than 0°C.

Table 6.2: Plates, sections and forgings for cargo tanks, secondary barriers and process pressure vessels for design temperatures below 0°C and down to −55°C.

Table 6.3: Plates, sections and forgings for cargo tanks, secondary barriers and process pressure vessels for design temperatures below −55°C and down to −165°C.

Table 6.4: Pipes (seamless and welded), forgings and castings for cargo and process piping for design temperatures below 0°C and down to −165°C.

Table 6.5: Plates and sections for hull structures required by 4.9.1 and 4.9.4.

Table 6.1

Plates, pipes (seamless and welded),[1] sections and forgings for cargo tanks and process pressure vessels for design temperatures not lower than 0°C

CHEMICAL COMPOSITION AND HEAT TREATMENT

Carbon-manganese steel   Fully killed

Fine grain steel where thickness exceeds 20 mm

Small additions of alloying elements by agreement with the Administration

Composition limits to be approved by the Administration

Normalized, or quenched and tempered[2]

TENSILE AND TOUGHNESS (IMPACT) TEST REQUIREMENTS

Plates	Each "piece" to be tested
Sections and forgings	Batch test
Tensile properties	Specified minimum yield stress not to exceed 410 N/mm^2 [3]
Charpy V-notch test	
Plates	Transverse test pieces. Minimum average energy (E) 27 J
Sections and forgings	Longitudinal test pieces. Minimum average energy (E) 41 J
Test temperature	

Thickness t (mm)	Test temperature (°C)
$t \leqslant 20$	0
$20 < t \leqslant 40$	−20

[1] For seamless pipes and fittings normal practice applies. The use of longitudinally and spirally welded pipes should be specially approved by the Administration.

[2] A controlled rolling procedure may be used as an alternative to normalizing or quenching and tempering, subject to special approval by the Administration.

[3] Materials with specified minimum yield stress exceeding 410 N/mm^2 may be specially approved by the Administration. For these materials, particular attention should be given to the hardness of the weld and heat-affected zone.

Table 6.2

Plates, sections and forgings[1] for cargo tanks, secondary barriers and process pressure vessels for design temperatures below −0°C and down to −55°C
Maximum thickness 25 mm[2]

CHEMICAL COMPOSITION AND HEAT TREATMENT

Carbon-manganese steel   Fully killed   Aluminium treated fine grain steel

Chemical composition (ladle analysis)

C	Mn	Si	S	P
0.16% max.[3]	0.70-1.60%	0.10-0.50%	0.035% max.	0.035% max.

Optional additions: Alloys and grain refining elements may be generally in accordance with the following:

Ni	Cr	Mo	Cu	Nb	V
0.80% max.	0.25% max.	0.08% max.	0.35% max.	0.05% max.	0.10% max.

Normalized or quenched and tempered[4]

TENSILE AND TOUGHNESS (IMPACT) TEST REQUIREMENTS

Plates	Each "piece" to be tested
Sections and forgings	Batch test
Charpy V-notch test	Test temperature 5°C below the design temperature or −20°C whichever is lower
Plates	Transverse test pieces. Minimum average energy value (E) 27 J
Sections and forgings[1]	Longitudinal test pieces. Minimum average energy value (E) 41 J

Notes

[1] The Charpy V-notch and chemistry requirements for forgings may be specially considered by the Administration.

[2] For material thickness of more than 25 mm, Charpy V-notch tests should be conducted as follows:

Material thickness (mm)	Test temperature (°C)
25 < t ⩽ 30	10° below design temperature or −20° whichever is lower
30 < t ⩽ 35	15° below design temperature or −20° whichever is lower
35 < t ⩽ 40	20° below design temperature

The impact energy value should be in accordance with the table for the applicable type of test specimen. For material thickness of more than 40 mm, the Charpy V-notch values should be specially considered.

Materials for tanks and parts of tanks which are completely thermally stress relieved after welding may be tested at temperature 5°C below the design temperature or −20°C whichever is lower.

For thermally stress relieved reinforcements and other fittings, the test temperature should be the same as that required for the adjacent tank-shell thickness.

[3] By special agreement with the Administration, the carbon content may be increased to 0.18% maximum provided the design temperature is not lower than −40°C.

[4] A controlled rolling procedure may be used as an alternative to normalizing or quenching and tempering, subject to special approval by the Administration.

Guidance:

For materials exceeding 25 mm in thickness for which the test temperature is −60°C or lower, the application of specially treated steels or steels in accordance with table 6.3 may be necessary.

Table 6.3

Plates, sections and forgings[1] for cargo tanks, secondary barriers and process pressure vessels for design temperatures below −55°C and down to −165°C[2]		
Maximum thickness 25 mm[3]		
Minimum design temp. (°C)	Chemical composition[4] and heat treatment	Impact test temp. (°C)
−60	1.5% nickel steel – normalized	−65
−65	2.25% nickel steel – normalized or normalized and tempered[5]	−70
−90	3.5% nickel steel – normalized or normalized and tempered[5]	−95
−105	5% nickel steel – normalized or normalized and tempered[5, 6]	−110
−165	9% nickel steel – double normalized and tempered or quenched and tempered	−196
−165	Austenitic steels, such as types 304, 304L, 316, 316L, 321 and 347 solution treated[7]	−196
−165	Aluminium alloys; such as type 5083 annealed	Not required
−165	Austenitic Fe-Ni alloy (36% nickel) Heat treatment as agreed	Not required

TENSILE AND TOUGHNESS (IMPACT) TEST REQUIREMENTS

Plates	Each "piece" to be tested
Sections and forgings	Batch test
Charpy V-notch test	
Plates	Transverse test pieces. Minimum average energy value (E) 27 J
Sections and forgings	Longitudinal test pieces. Minimum average energy value (E) 41 J

[1] The impact test required for forgings used in critical applications should be subject to special consideration by the Administration.

[2] The requirements for design temperatures below −165°C should be specially agreed with the Administration.

[3] For materials 1.5% Ni, 2.25% Ni, 3.5% Ni and 5% Ni, with thicknesses greater than 25 mm, the impact tests should be conducted as follows:

Material thickness (mm)	Test temperature (°C)
$25 < t \leqslant 30$	10° below design temperature
$30 < t \leqslant 35$	15° below design temperature
$35 < t \leqslant 40$	20° below design temperature

In no case should the test temperature be above that indicated in the table.

The energy value should be in accordance with the table for the applicable type of test specimen. For material thickness of more than 40 mm, the Charpy V-notch values should be specially considered.

For 9% Ni, austenitic stainless steels and aluminium alloys, thicknesses greater than 25 mm may be used at the discretion of the Administration.

[4] The chemical composition limits should be approved by the Administration.

[5] A lower minimum design temperature for quenched and tempered steels may be specially agreed with the Administration.

[6] A specially heat treated 5% nickel steel, for example triple heat treated 5% nickel steel, may be used down to −165°C upon special agreement with the Administration, provided that the impact tests are carried out at −196°C.

[7] The impact test may be omitted subject to agreement with the Administration.

Table 6.4

Pipes (seamless and welded[1]), forgings[2] and castings[2] for cargo and process piping for design temperatures below 0° and down to −165°C[3]			
Maximum thickness 25mm			
Minimum design temp. (°C)	Chemical composition[5] and heat treatment	Impact test	
		Test temp. (°C)	Minimum average energy (E) (J)
−55	Carbon-manganese steel. Fully killed fine grain. Normalized or as agreed[6]	[4]	27
−65	2.25% nickel steel. Normalized or normalized and tempered[6]	−70	34
−90	3.5% nickel steel. Normalized or normalized and tempered[6]	−95	34
−165	9% nickel steel.[7] Double normalized and tempered or quenched and tempered	− 196	41
	Austenitic steels, such as types 304, 304L, 316, 316L, 321 and 347. Solution treated[8]	−196	41
	Aluminium alloys, such as type 5083 annealed		Not required
TENSILE AND TOUGHNESS (IMPACT) TEST REQUIREMENTS Each batch to be tested Impact test Longitudinal test pieces			

Notes

[1] The use of longitudinally or spirally welded pipes should be specially approved by the Administration.

[2] The requirements for forgings and castings may be subject to special consideration by the Administration.

[3] The requirements for design temperatures below −165°C should be specially agreed with the Administration.

[4] The test temperature should be 5°C below the design temperature or −20°C whichever is lower.

[5] The composition limits should be approved by the Administration.

[6] A lower design temperature may be specially agreed with the Administration for quenched and tempered materials.

[7] This chemical composition is not suitable for castings.

[8] Impact tests may be omitted subject to agreement with the Administration.

Table 6.5

Plates and sections for hull structures required by 4.9.1 and 4.9.4							
Minimum design temperature of hull structure (°C)	Maximum thickness (mm) for steel grades in accordance with 6.1.9						
	A	B	D	E	AH	DH	EH
0 and above[1] −5 and above[2]	Normal practice						
down to −5	15	25	30	50	25	45	50
down to −10	x	20	25	50	20	40	50
down to −20	x	x	20	50	x	30	50
down to − 30	x	x	x	40	x	20	40
Below −30	In accordance with table 6.2 except that the thickness limitation given in table 6.2 and in footnote 2 of that table does not apply.						

Notes

"x" means steel grade not to be used.

[1] For the purpose of 4.9.4.

[2] For the purpose of 4.9.1.

6.3 Welding and non-destructive testing

6.3.1 *General*

The requirements of this section are those generally employed for carbon, carbon-manganese, nickel alloy and stainless steels, and may form the basis for acceptance testing of other material. At the discretion of the Administration, impact testing of stainless steel and aluminium alloy weldments may be omitted and other tests may be specially required for any material.

6.3.2 *Welding consumables*

Welding consumables intended for welding of cargo tanks should be in accordance with Recognized Standards unless otherwise agreed with the

Administration. Deposited weld metal tests and butt weld tests should be required for all welding consumables, unless otherwise specially agreed with the Administration. The results obtained from tensile and Charpy V-notch impact tests should be in accordance with Recognized Standards. The chemical composition of the deposited weld metal should be recorded for information and approval.

6.3.3 Welding procedure tests for cargo tanks and process pressure vessels

6.3.3.1 Welding procedure tests for cargo tanks and process pressure vessels are required for all butt welds and the test assemblies should be representative of:

- each base material

- each type of consumable and welding process

- each welding position.

For butt welds in plates, the test assemblies should be so prepared that the rolling direction is parallel to the direction of welding. The range of thickness qualified by each welding procedure test should be in accordance with Recognized Standards. Radiographic or ultrasonic testing may be performed at the option of the fabricator or the Administration. Procedure tests for consumables intended for fillet welding should be in accordance with Recognized Standards. In such cases consumables should be selected which exhibit satisfactory impact properties.

6.3.3.2 The following welding procedure tests for cargo tanks and process pressure vessels should be made from each test assembly:

.1 Cross-weld tensile tests.

.2 Transverse bend tests which may be face, root or side bends at the discretion of the Administration. However, longitudinal bend tests may be required in lieu of transverse bend tests in cases where the base material and weld metal have different strength levels.

.3 One set of three Charpy V-notch impacts, generally at each of the following locations, as shown in figure 6.1:

- Centreline of the welds

- Fusion line (FL)

- 1 mm from the FL

- 3 mm from the FL

- 5 mm from the FL

.4   Macrosection, microsection and hardness survey may also be required by the Administration.

6.3.4 *Test requirements*

6.3.4.1 *Tensile tests:* Generally, tensile strength should not be less than the specified minimum tensile strength for the appropriate parent materials. The Administration may also require that the transverse weld tensile strength should not be less than the specified tensile strength for the weld metal, where the weld metal has a lower tensile strength than that of the parent metal. In every case, the position of fracture is to be reported for information.

6.3.4.2 *Bend tests:* No fracture is acceptable after a 180° bend over a former of a diameter four times the thickness of the test pieces, unless otherwise specially required by or agreed with the Administration.

6.3.4.3 *Charpy V-notch impact tests:* Charpy tests should be conducted at the temperature prescribed for the base material being joined. The results of weld metal impacts tests, minimum average energy (E), should be no less than 27 J. The weld metal requirements for subsize specimens and single energy values should be in accordance with 6.1.4. The results of fusion line and heat affected zone impact tests should show a minimum average energy (E) in accordance with the transverse or longitudinal requirements of the base material, whichever is applicable, and for subsize specimens, the minimum average energy (E) should be in accordance with 6.1.4. If the material thickness does not permit machining either full-size or standard subsize specimens, the testing procedure and acceptance standards should be in accordance with Recognized Standards.

6.3.5 *Welding procedure tests for piping*

Welding procedure tests for piping should be carried out and should be similar to those detailed for cargo tanks in 6.3.3. Unless otherwise specially agreed with the Administration, the test requirements should be in accordance with 6.3.4.

6.3.6 *Production weld tests*

6.3.6.1 For all cargo tanks and process pressure vessels except integral and membrane tanks, production weld tests should generally be performed for approximately each 50 m of butt-weld joints and should be representative of each welding position. For secondary barriers, the same type production tests as required for primary tanks should be performed except that the number of tests may be reduced subject to agreement with the Administration. Tests, other than those specified in 6.3.6.2, .3 and .4, may be required for cargo tanks or secondary barriers at the discretion of the Administration.

6.3.6.2 The production tests for types A and B independent tanks and semi-membrane tanks should include the following tests:

.1 Bend tests, and where required for procedure tests one set of three Charpy V-notch tests should be made for each 50 m of weld. The Charpy V-notch tests should be made with specimens having the notch alternately located in the centre of the weld and in the heat affected zone (most critical location based on procedure qualification results). For austenitic stainless steel, all notches should be in the centre of the weld.

.2 The test requirements are the same as the applicable test requirements listed in 6.3.4 except that impact tests that do not meet the prescribed energy requirements may still be accepted, upon special consideration by the Administration, by passing a drop weight test. In such cases, two drop weight specimens should be tested for each set of Charpy specimens that failed and both must show "no break" performance at the temperature at which the Charpy tests were conducted.

6.3.6.3 In addition to those tests listed in 6.3.6.2.1 for type C independent tanks and process pressure vessels, transverse weld tensile tests are required. The test requirements are listed in 6.3.4 except that impact tests that do not meet the prescribed energy requirements may still be accepted upon special consideration by the Administration, by passing a drop weight test. In such cases, two drop weight specimens should be tested for each set of Charpy specimens that failed, and both must show "no break" performance at the temperature at which the Charpy tests were conducted.

6.3.6.4 Production tests for integral and membrane tanks should be in accordance with Recognized Standards.

6.3.7 Non-destructive testing

6.3.7.1 For type A independent tanks and semi-membrane tanks where the design temperature is −20°C or less, and for type B independent tanks regardless of temperature, all full penetration butt welds of the shell plating of cargo tanks should be subjected to 100% radiographic inspection.

6.3.7.1.1 Where the design temperature is higher than −20°C, all full penetration butt welds in way of intersections and at least 10% of the remaining full penetration welds of tank structures should be subjected to radiographic inspection.

6.3.7.1.2 In each case the remaining tank structure including the welding of stiffeners and other fittings and attachments should be examined by magnetic particle or dye penetrant methods as considered necessary by the Administration.

6.3.7.1.3 All test procedures and acceptance standards should be in accordance with Recognized Standards. The Administration may accept an approved ultrasonic test procedure in lieu of radiographic inspection, but may in addition require supplementary inspection by radiography at selected locations. Further, the Administration may require ultrasonic testing in addition to normal radiographic inspection.

6.3.7.2 Inspection of type C independent tanks and process pressure vessels should be carried out in accordance with 4.10.9.

6.3.7.3 For integral and membrane tanks, special weld inspection procedures and acceptance criteria should be in accordance with Recognized Standards.

6.3.7.4 The inspection and non-destructive testing of the inner hull or the independent tank structures supporting internal insulation tanks should take into account the design criteria given in 4.4.7. The schedule for inspection and non-destructive testing should be to the satisfaction of the Administration.

6.3.7.5 Inspection of piping should be carried out in accordance with the requirements of chapter 5.

6.3.7.6 The secondary barrier should be radiographed as considered necessary by the Administration. Where the outer shell of the hull is part of the secondary barrier, all sheer strake butts and the intersections of all butts and seams in the side shell should be tested by radiography.

Chapter 7

Cargo pressure/temperature control

7.1 General

7.1.1 Unless the entire cargo system is designed to withstand the full gauge vapour pressure of the cargo under conditions of the upper ambient design temperatures, maintenance of the cargo tank pressure below the MARVS should be provided by one or more of the following means, except as otherwise provided in this section:

.1 a system which regulates the pressure in the cargo tanks by the use of mechanical refrigeration;

.2 a system whereby the boil-off vapours are utilized as fuel for shipboard use or waste heat system subject to the provisions of chapter 16. This system may be used at all times, including while in port and while manoeuvring, provided that a means of disposing of excess energy is provided, such as a steam dump system, that is satisfactory to the Administration;

.3 a system allowing the product to warm up and increase in pressure. The insulation or cargo tank design pressure or both should be adequate to provide for a suitable margin for the operating time and temperatures involved. The system should be acceptable to the Administration in each case;

.4 other systems acceptable to the Administration;

.5 in addition to the above means, the Administration may permit certain cargoes to be controlled by venting cargo vapours to the atmosphere at sea. This may also be permitted in port with the permission of the port Administration.

7.1.2 The systems required by 7.1.1 should be constructed, fitted and tested to the satisfaction of the Administration. Materials used in their construction should be suitable for use with the cargoes to be carried. For normal service, the upper ambient design temperature should be:

sea: 32°C
air: 45°C

For service in especially hot or cold zones these design temperatures should be increased or reduced, as appropriate, by the Administration.

7.1.3 For certain highly dangerous cargoes specified in chapter 17, the cargo containment system should be capable of withstanding the full vapour pressure of the cargo under conditions of the upper ambient design temperatures irrespective of any system provided for dealing with boil-off gas.

7.2 Refrigeration systems

7.2.1 A refrigeration system should consist of one or more units capable of maintaining the required cargo pressure/temperature under conditions of the upper ambient design temperatures. Unless an alternative means of controlling the cargo pressure/temperature is provided to the satisfaction of the Administration, a stand-by unit (or units) affording space capacity at least equal to the largest required single unit should be provided. A stand-by unit should consist of a compressor with its driving motor, control system and any necessary fittings to permit operation independently of the normal service units. A stand-by heat exchanger should be provided unless the normal heat exchanger for the unit has an excess capacity of at least 25% of the largest required capacity. Separate piping systems are not required.

7.2.2.1 Where two or more refrigerated cargoes which may react chemically in a dangerous manner are carried simultaneously, special consideration should be given to the refrigeration systems to avoid the possibility of mixing cargoes. For the carriage of such cargoes, separate refrigeration systems, each complete with a stand-by unit as specified in 7.2.1, should be provided for each cargo. However, where cooling is provided by an indirect or combined system and leakage in the heat exchangers cannot cause mixing of the cargoes under any envisaged condition, separate refrigeration units need not be fitted.

7.2.2.2 Where two or more refrigerated cargoes are not mutually soluble under the conditions of carriage, so that their vapour pressures would be additive on mixing, special consideration should be given to the refrigeration systems to avoid the possibility of mixing cargoes.

7.2.3 Where cooling water is required in refrigeration systems, an adequate supply should be provided by a pump or pumps used exclusively for this purpose. This pump or these pumps should have at least two sea suction lines, where practicable leading from sea-chests, one port and one starboard. A spare pump of adequate capacity should be provided, which may be a pump used for other services so long as its use for cooling would not interfere with any other essential service.

7.2.4 The refrigeration system may be arranged in one of the following ways:

.1 a direct system where evaporated cargo is compressed, condensed and returned to cargo tanks. For certain cargoes specified in chapter 17 this system should not be used;

.2 an indirect system where cargo or evaporated cargo is cooled or condensed by refrigerant without being compressed;

.3 a combined system where evaporated cargo is compressed and condensed in a cargo/refrigerant heat exchanger and returned to the cargo tanks. For certain cargoes specified in chapter 17 this system should not be used.

7.2.5 All primary and secondary refrigerants must be compatible with each other and with the cargo with which they come into contact. The heat exchange may take place either remotely from the cargo tank or by cooling coils fitted inside or outside the cargo tank.

Chapter 8

Cargo tank vent systems

8.1 General

All cargo tanks should be provided with a pressure relief system appropriate to the design of the cargo containment system and the cargo being carried. Hold spaces, interbarrier spaces and cargo piping which may be subject to pressures beyond their design capabilities should also be provided with a suitable pressure relief system. The pressure relief system should be connected to a vent piping system so designed as to minimize the possibility of cargo vapour accumulating on the decks, or entering accommodation spaces, service spaces, control stations and machinery spaces, or other spaces where it may create a dangerous condition. Pressure control systems specified by chapter 7 should be independent of the pressure relief systems.

8.2 Pressure relief systems

8.2.1 Each cargo tank with a volume exceeding 20 m³ should be fitted with at least two pressure relief valves of approximately equal capacity, suitably designed and constructed for the prescribed service. For cargo tanks with a volume not exceeding 20 m³, a single relief valve may be fitted.

8.2.2 Interbarrier spaces should be provided with pressure relief devices to the satisfaction of the Administration.

8.2.3 The setting of the pressure relief valves should not be higher than the vapour pressure which has been used in the design of the tank.

8.2.4 Pressure relief valves should be connected to the highest part of the cargo tank above deck level. Pressure relief valves on cargo tanks with a design temperature below 0°C should be arranged to prevent their becoming inoperative due to ice formation when they are closed. Due consideration should be given to the construction and arrangement of pressure relief valves on cargo tanks subject to low ambient temperatures.

8.2.5 Pressure relieve valves should be prototype tested to ensure that the valves have the capacity required. Each valve should be tested to ensure that it opens at the prescribed pressure setting with an allowance not exceeding ± 10% for 0 to 1.5 bar, ± 6% for 1.5 to 3.0 bar, ± 3% for 3.0 bar and above. Pressure relief valves should be set and sealed by a competent authority acceptable to the Administration and a record of this action, including the values of set pressure, should be retained aboard the ship.

8.2.6 In the case of cargo tanks permitted to have more than one relief valve setting this may be accomplished by:

.1 installing two or more properly set and sealed valves and providing means as necessary for isolating the valves not in use from the cargo tank; or

.2 installing relief valves whose settings may be changed by the insertion of previously approved spacer pieces or alternative springs or by other similar means not requiring pressure testing to verify the new set pressure. All other valve adjustments should be sealed.

8.2.7 The changing of the set pressure under the provisions of 8.2.6 should be carried out under the supervision of the master in accordance with procedures approved by Administration and specified in the ship's operating manual. Changes in set pressures should be recorded in the ship's log and a sign posted in the cargo control room, if provided, and at each relief valve, stating the set pressure.

8.2.8 Stop valves or other means of blanking off pipes between tanks and pressure relief valves to facilitate maintenance should not be fitted unless all the following arrangements are provided:

.1 suitable arrangements to prevent more than one pressure relief valve being out of service at the same time;

.2 a device which automatically and in a clearly visible way indicates which one of the pressure relief valves is out of service; and

.3 pressure relief valve capacities such that if one valve is out of service the remaining valves have the combined relieving capacity required by 8.5. However, this capacity may be provided by the combined capacity of all valves, if a suitably maintained spare valve is carried on board.

8.2.9 Each pressure relief valve installed on a cargo tank should be connected to a venting system, which should be so constructed that the discharge of gas will be directed upwards and so arranged as to minimize the possibility of water or snow entering the vent system. The height of vent exits should be not less than $B/3$ or 6 m, whichever is greater, above the weather deck and 6 m above the working area and the fore and aft gangway.

8.2.10 Cargo tank pressure relief valve vent exits should be arranged at a distance at least equal to B or 25 m, whichever is less, from the nearest air intake or opening to accommodation spaces, service spaces and control stations, or other gas-safe spaces. For ships less than 90 m in length, smaller distances may be permitted by the Administration. All other vent exits connected to the cargo containment system should be arranged at a distance of at least 10 m from the nearest air intake or opening to accommodation spaces, service spaces and control stations, or other gas-safe spaces.

8.2.11 All other cargo vent exits not dealt with in other chapters should be arranged in accordance with 8.2.9 and 8.2.10.

8.2.12 If cargoes which react in a hazardous manner with each other are carried simultaneously, a separate pressure relief system should be fitted for each cargo carried.

8.2.13 In the vent piping system, means for draining liquid from places where it may accumulate should be provided. The pressure relief valves and piping should be so arranged that liquid can under no circumstances accumulate in or·near the pressure relief valves.

8.2.14 Suitable protection screens should be fitted on vent outlets to prevent the ingress of foreign objects.

8.2.15 All vent piping should be so designed and arranged that it will not be damaged by temperature variations to which it may be exposed, or by the ship's motions.

8.2.16 The back pressure in the vent lines from the pressure relief valves should be taken into account in determining the flow capacity required by 8.5.

8.2.17 Pressure relief valves should be positioned on the cargo tank so that they will remain in the vapour phase under conditions of 15° list and 0.015L trim, where L is defined in 1.3.23.

8.3 Additional pressure relieving system for liquid level control

8.3.1 Where required by 15.1.4.2, an additional pressure relieving system to prevent the tank from becoming liquid full at any time during relief under the fire exposure conditions referred to in 8.5 should be fitted to each tank. This pressure relieving system should consist of:

> .1 one or more relief valves set at a pressure corresponding to the gauge vapour pressure of the cargo at the reference temperature defined in 15.1.4.2; and
>
> .2 an override arrangement, whenever necessary, to prevent its normal operation. This arrangement should include fusible elements designed to melt at temperatures between 98°C and 104°C and to cause relief valves specified in 8.3.1.1 to become operable. The fusible elements should be located, in particular, in the vicinity of relief valves. The system should become operable upon loss of system power if provided. The override arrangement should not be dependent on any source of ship's power.

8.3.2 The total relieving capacity of the additional pressure relieving system at the pressure mentioned in 8.3.1.1 should not be less than:

$$Q' = FG'A^{0.82} \quad (m^3/s)$$

where:

Q' = minimum required rate of discharge of air at standard conditions of 273 K and 1.013 bar.

$$G' = \frac{12.4}{(L + \rho_r m)D} \sqrt{\frac{ZT'}{M}}$$

with:

ρ_r = relative density of liquid phase of product at relieving conditions (ρ_r = 1.0 for fresh water).

m = $-di/d\rho_r$ = gradient of decrease of liquid phase enthalpy against increase of liquid phase density (kJ/kg) at relieving conditions. For set pressures not higher than 2.0 bar the values in table 8.1 may be used. For products not listed in the table and for higher set pressures, the value of m should be calculated on the basis of the thermodynamic data of the product itself;

i = enthalpy of liquid (kJ/kg);

T' = temperature in kelvins (K) at relieving conditions, i.e. at the pressure at which the additional pressure relieving system is set;

F, A, L, D, Z and M are defined in 8.5.2.

Table 8.1 – Factor (m)

Product	$m = -di/d\rho_r$ (kJ/kg)
Ammonia, anhydrous	3,400
Butadiene	1,800
Butane	2,000
Butylenes	1,900
Ethane	2,100
Ethylene	1,500
Methane	2,300
Methyl chloride	816
Nitrogen	400
Propane	2,000
Propylene	1,600
Propylene oxide	1,550
Vinyl chloride	900

The values in this table may be used for set pressures not higher than 2.0 bar.

8.3.3 Compliance with 8.3.1.1 requires changing of the setting of the relief valves provided for in this section. This should be accomplished in accordance with the provisions of 8.2.6 and 8.2.7.

8.3.4 Relief valves mentioned under 8.3.1.1 above may be the same as the pressure relief valves mentioned in 8.2, provided the setting pressure and the relieving capacity are in compliance with the requirements of this section.

8.3.5 The exhaust of such pressure relief valves may be led to the venting system referred to in 8.2.9. If separate venting arrangements are fitted these should be in accordance with the requirements of 8.2.9 to 8.2.15.

8.4 Vacuum protection systems

8.4.1 Cargo tanks designed to withstand a maximum external pressure differential exceeding 0.25 bar and capable of withstanding the maximum external pressure differential which can be attained at maximum discharge rates with no vapour return into the cargo tanks, or by operation of a cargo refrigeration system, need no vacuum relief protection.

8.4.2 Cargo tanks designed to withstand a maximum external pressure differential not exceeding 0.25 bar, or tanks which cannot withstand the maximum external pressure differential that can be attained at maximum discharge rates with no vapour return into the cargo tanks, or by operation of a cargo refrigeration system, or by sending boil-off vapour to the machinery spaces, should be fitted with:

.1 two independent pressure switches to sequentially alarm and subsequently stop all suction of cargo liquid or vapour from the cargo tank, and refrigeration equipment if fitted, by suitable means at a pressure sufficiently below the maximum external designed pressure differential of the cargo tank; or

.2 vacuum relief valves with a gas flow capacity at least equal to the maximum cargo discharge rate per cargo tank, set to open at a pressure sufficiently below the external design differential pressure of the cargo tank; or

.3 other vacuum relief systems acceptable to the Administration.

8.4.3 Subject to the requirements of chapter 17, the vacuum relief valves should admit an inert gas, cargo vapour or air to the cargo tank and should be arranged to minimize the possibility of the entrance of water or snow. If cargo vapour is admitted, it should be from a source other than the cargo vapour lines.

8.4.4 The vacuum protection system should be capable of being tested to ensure that it operates at the prescribed pressure.

8.5 Size of valves

Pressure relief valves should have a combined relieving capacity for each cargo tank to discharge the greater of the following with not more than a 20% rise in cargo tank pressure above the MARVS:

.1 the maximum capacity of the cargo tank inerting system if the maximum attainable working pressure of the cargo tank inerting system exceeds the MARVS of the cargo tanks; or

.2 vapours generated under fire exposure computed using the following formula:

$$Q = FGA^{0.82} \ (m^3/s)$$

where:

Q = minimum required rate of discharge of air at standard conditions of 273 K and 1.013 bar.

F = fire exposure factor for different cargo tank types:

F = 1.0 for tanks without insulation located on deck;

F = 0.5 for tanks above the deck when insulation is approved by the Administration. (Approval will be based on the use of an approved fireproofing material, the thermal conductance of insulation, and its stability under fire exposure);

F = 0.5 for uninsulated independent tanks installed in holds;

F = 0.2 for insulated independent tanks in holds (or uninsulated independent tanks in insulated holds);

F = 0.1 for insulated independent tanks in inerted holds (or uninsulated independent tanks in inerted, insulated holds);

F = 0.1 for membrane and semi-membrane tanks.

For independent tanks partly protruding through the open deck, the fire exposure factor should be determined on the basis of the surface areas above and below deck.

G = gas factor

$$G = \frac{12.4}{LD} \sqrt{\frac{ZT}{M}}$$

with:

T = temperature in kelvins (K) at relieving conditions, i.e. 120% of the pressure at which the pressure relief valve is set;

L = latent heat of the material being vaporized at relieving conditions, in kJ/kg;

D = constant based on relation of specific heats k, shown in table 8.2; if k is not known, D = 0.606 should be used. The constant D may also be calculated by the following formula:

$$D = \sqrt{k\left(\frac{2}{k+1}\right)^{\frac{k+1}{k-1}}}$$

$\cdot Z$ = compressibility factor of the gas at relieving conditions; if not known, Z = 1.0 should be used.

M = molecular mass of the product.

A = external surface area of the tank (m²) for different tank types:

for body-of-revolution type tanks:

A = external surface area;

for other than body-of-revolution type tanks:

A = external surface area less the projected bottom surface area;

for tanks consisting of an array of pressure vessel tanks:

insulation on the ship's structure:

A = external surface area of the hold less its projected area;

insulation on the tank structure

A = external surface area of the array of pressure vessels excluding insulation, less the projected bottom area as shown in figure 8.1.

Table 8.2 – Constant D

k	D	k	D
1.00	0.606	1.52	0.704
1.02	0.611	1.54	0.707
1.04	0.615	1.56	0.710
1.06	0.620	1.58	0.713
1.08	0.624	1.60	0.716
1.10	0.628	1.62	0.719
1.12	0.633	1.64	0.722
1.14	0.637	1.66	0.725
1.16	0.641	1.68	0.728
1.18	0.645	1.70	0.731
1.20	0.649	1.72	0.734
1.22	0.652	1.74	0.736
1.24	0.656	1.76	0.739
1.26	0.660	1.78	0.742
1.28	0.664	1.80	0.745
1.30	0.667	1.82	0.747
1.32	0.671	1.84	0.750
1.34	0.674	1.86	0.752
1.36	0.677	1.88	0.755
1.38	0.681	1.90	0.758
1.40	0.685	1.92	0.760
1.42	0.688	1.94	0.763
1.44	0.691	1.96	0.765
1.46	0.695	1.98	0.767
1.48	0.698	2.00	0.770
1.50	0.701	2.02	0.772
		2.20	0.792

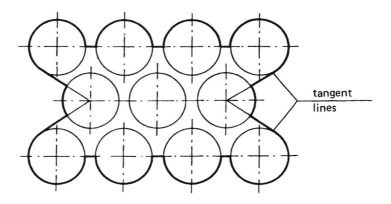

Figure 8.1

Chapter 9

Environmental control

9.1 Environmental control within cargo tanks and cargo piping systems

9.1.1 A piping system should be provided to enable each cargo tank to be safely gas-freed, and to be safely purged with cargo gas from a gas-free condition. The system should be arranged to minimize the possibility of pockets of gas or air remaining after gas-freeing or purging.

9.1.2 A sufficient number of gas sampling points should be provided for each cargo tank in order to adequately monitor the progress of purging and gas-freeing. Gas sampling connections should be valved and capped above the main deck.

9.1.3 For flammable gases, the system should be arranged to minimize the possibility of a flammable mixture existing in the cargo tank during any part of the gas-freeing operation by utilizing an inerting medium as an intermediate step. In addition, the system should enable the cargo tank to be purged with an inerting medium prior to filling with cargo vapour or liquid, without permitting a flammable mixture to exist at any time within the cargo tank.

9.1.4 Piping systems which may contain cargo should be capable of being gas-freed and purged as provided in 9.1.1 and 9.1.3.

9.1.5 Inert gas utilized in these procedures may be provided from the shore or from the ship.

9.2 Environmental control within the hold spaces (cargo containment systems other than type C independent tanks)

9.2.1 Interbarrier and hold spaces associated with cargo containment systems for flammable gases requiring full secondary barriers should be inerted with a suitable dry inert gas and kept inerted with make-up gas provided by a shipboard inert gas generation system, or by shipboard storage which should be sufficient for normal consumption for at least 30 days.

9.2.2.1 Interbarrier and hold spaces associated with cargo containment systems for flammable gases requiring partial secondary barriers should be inerted with suitable dry inert gas and kept inerted with make-up gas provided by a shipboard inert gas generation system or by shipboard storage which should be sufficient for normal consumption for at least 30 days.

9.2.2.2 Alternatively, subject to the restrictions specified in chapter 17, the Administration may allow the spaces referred to in 9.2.2.1 to be filled with dry air provided that the ship maintains a stored charge of inert gas or is fitted with an inert gas generation system sufficient to inert the largest of these spaces; and provided that the configuration of the spaces and the relevant vapour detection systems, together with the capability of the inerting arrangements, ensure that any leakage from the cargo tanks will be rapidly detected and inerting effected before a dangerous condition can develop. Equipment for the provision of sufficient dry air of suitable quality to satisfy the expected demand should be provided.

9.2.3 For non-flammable gases, the spaces referred to in 9.2.1 and 9.2.2.1 may be maintained with a suitable dry air or inert atmosphere.

9.2.4 In case of internal insulation tanks, environmental control arrangements are not required for interbarrier spaces and spaces between the secondary barrier and the inner hull or independent tank structures completely filled with insulation materials complying with 4.9.7.2.

9.3 Environmental control of spaces surrounding type C independent tanks

Spaces surrounding refrigerated cargo tanks not having secondary barriers should be filled with suitable dry inert gas or dry air and be maintained in this condition with make-up inert gas provided by a shipboard inert gas generation system, shipboard storage of inert gas, or dry air provided by suitable air drying equipment.

9.4 Inerting

9.4.1 Inerting refers to the process of providing a non-combustible environment by the addition of compatible gases, which may be carried in storage vessels or produced on board the ship or supplied from the shore. The inert gases should be compatible chemically and operationally, at all temperatures likely to occur within the spaces to be inerted, with the materials of construction of the spaces and the cargo. The dew points of the gases should be taken into consideration.

9.4.2 Where inert gas is also stored for fire-fighting purposes, it should be carried in separate containers and should not be used for cargo services.

9.4.3 Where inert gas is stored at temperatures below 0°C, either as a liquid or as a vapour, the storage and supply system should be so designed that the temperature of the ship's structure is not reduced below the limiting values imposed on it.

9.4.4 Arrangements suitable for the cargo carried should be provided to prevent the backflow of cargo vapour into the inert gas system.

9.4.5 The arrangements should be such that each space being inerted can be isolated and the necessary controls and relief valves etc. should be provided for controlling pressure in these spaces.

9.5 Inert gas production on board

9.5.1 The equipment should be capable of producing inert gas with an oxygen content at no time greater than 5% by volume subject to the special requirements of chapter 17. A continuous-reading oxygen content meter should be fitted to the inert gas supply from the equipment and should be fitted with an alarm set at a maximum of 5% oxygen content by volume subject to the requirements of chapter 17. Additionally, where inert gas is made by an on-board process of fractional distillation of air which involves the storage of the cryogenic liquefied nitrogen for subsequent release, the liquefied gas entering the storage vessel should be monitored for traces of oxygen to avoid possible initial high oxygen enrichment of the gas when released for inerting purposes.

9.5.2 An inert gas system should have pressure controls and monitoring arrangements appropriate to the cargo containment system. A means acceptable to the Administration, located in the cargo area, of preventing the backflow of cargo gas should be provided.

9.5.3 Spaces containing inert gas generation plants should have no direct access to accommodation spaces, service spaces or control stations, but may be located in machinery spaces. If such plants are located in machinery spaces or other spaces outside the cargo area, two non-return valves or equivalent devices should be fitted in the inert gas main in the cargo area as required in 9.5.2. Inert gas piping should not pass through accommodation spaces, service spaces or control stations.

9.5.4 Flame burning equipment for generating inert gas should not be located within the cargo area. Special consideration may be given to the location of inert gas generating equipment using the catalytic combustion process.

Chapter 10

Electrical installations

10.1 General

10.1.1 The provisions of this chapter are applicable to ships carrying flammable products and should be applied in conjunction with part D of chapter 11-1 of the 1983 SOLAS amendments.

10.1.2 Electrical installations should be such as to minimize the risk of fire and explosion from flammable products. Electrical installations complying with this chapter need not be considered as a source of ignition for the purposes of chapter 3.

10.1.3 Administrations should take appropriate steps to ensure uniformity in the implementation and application of the provisions of this chapter in respect of electrical installations.*

10.1.4 Electrical equipment or wiring should not be installed in gas-dangerous spaces or zones unless essential for operational purposes, when the exceptions listed in 10.2 are permitted.

10.1.5 Where electrical equipment is installed in gas-dangerous spaces or zones as provided in 10.1.4, it should be to the satisfaction of the Administration and approved by the relevant authorities recognized by the Administration for operation in the flammable atmosphere concerned.

10.2 Types of equipment

Certified safe type equipment may be fitted in gas-dangerous spaces and zones in accordance with the following provisions:

10.2.1 *Gas-dangerous spaces and zones, general*

Intrinsically safe electrical equipment and wiring may be fitted in all gas-dangerous spaces and zones as defined in 1.3.17.

---

* Refer to the Recommendations published by the International Electrotechnical Commission and in particular to *Publication 92-502.*

10.2.2 *Cargo containment systems*

Submerged cargo pump motors and their supply cables may be fitted in cargo containment systems. Arrangements should be made to automatically shut down the motors in the event of low liquid level. This may be accomplished by sensing low pump discharge pressure, low motor current, or low liquid level. This shutdown should be alarmed at the cargo control station. Cargo pump motors should be capable of being isolated from their electrical supply during gas-freeing operations.

10.2.3 *Hold spaces and certain other spaces*

10.2.3.1 In hold spaces where cargo is carried in a cargo containment system requiring a secondary barrier, supply cables for submerged cargo pump motors may be installed.

10.2.3.2 In hold spaces where cargo is carried in a cargo containment system not requiring a secondary barrier and in spaces described in 1.3.17.5, the following may be installed:

  .1 through runs of cables;

  .2 lighting fittings with pressurized enclosures or of the flameproof type. The lighting system should be divided between at least two branch circuits. All switches and protective devices should interrupt all poles or phases and be located in a gas-safe space; and

  .3 electrical depth sounding or log devices and impressed current cathodic protection system anodes or electrodes. These devices should be housed in gastight enclosures;

and only in spaces described in 1.3.17.5:

  .4 flameproof motors for valve operation for cargo or ballast systems; and

  .5 flameproof general alarm audible indicators.

10.2.4 *Cargo pump and cargo compressor rooms*

10.2.4.1 Lighting fittings should have pressurized enclosures or should be of the flameproof type. The lighting system should be divided between at least two branch circuits. All switches and protective devices should interrupt all poles or phases and be located in a gas-safe space.

10.2.4.2 Electric motors for driving cargo pumps or cargo compressors should be separated from these spaces by a gastight bulkhead or deck. Flexible couplings or other means of maintaining alignment should be fitted to the shafts between the driven equipment and its motors and, in addition, suitable glands should be provided where the shafts pass through the gastight bulkhead or deck. Such electric motors and associated equipment should be located in a compartment complying with chapter 12.

10.2.4.3 Where operational or structural requirements are such as to make it impossible to comply with the method described in 10.2.4.2, motors of the following certified safety types may be installed:

.1   increased safety type with flameproof enclosure; and

.2   pressurized type.

10.2.4.4 General alarm audible indicators should have flameproof enclosures.

10.2.5 *Zones on open decks, spaces other than hold spaces*

10.2.5.1 In zones on open decks or non-enclosed spaces on the open deck, with 3 m of any cargo tank outlet, gas or vapour outlet, cargo pipe flange, cargo valves or entrances and ventilation openings to cargo pump rooms and cargo compressor rooms; in zones on the open deck over the cargo area and 3 m forward and aft of the cargo area on the open deck and up to a height of 2.4 m above the deck; in zones within 2.4 m of the outer surface of a cargo containment system where such surface is exposed to the weather the following may be installed:

.1   certified safe type equipment; and

.2   through runs of cables.

10.2.5.2 In enclosed or semi-enclosed spaces in which pipes containing cargoes are located and in compartments for cargo hoses the following may be installed:

.1   lighting fittings with pressurized enclosures, or of the flameproof type. The lighting system should be divided between at least two branch circuits. All switches and protective devices should interrupt all poles or phases and be located in a gas-safe space; and

.2   through runs of cables.

10.2.5.3 In enclosed or semi-enclosed spaces having a direct opening into any gas-dangerous space or zone there should be installed electrical installations complying with the requirements for the space or zone to which the opening leads.

10.2.5.4 Electrical equipment within spaces protected by airlocks should be of the certified safe type unless arranged to be de-energized by measures required by 3.6.4.

Chapter 11

Fire protection and fire extinction

11.1 Fire safety requirements

11.1.1 The requirements for tankers in chapter II-2 of the 1983 SOLAS amendments should apply to ships covered by the Code, irrespective of tonnage including ships of less than 500 tons gross tonnage, except that:

.1   regulation 56.6 does not apply;

.2   regulation 4 as applicable to cargo ships and regulation 7 should apply as they would apply to tankers of 2,000 tons gross tonnage and over;

.3   the following regulations of chapter II-2 of the 1983 SOLAS amendments related to tankers do not apply and are replaced by chapters and sections of the Code as detailed below:

Regulation	Replaced by
17	11.6
56.1 and 56.2	chapter 3
60, 61, 62	11.3 and 11.4
63	11.5

11.1.2 All sources of ignition should be excluded from spaces where flammable vapour may be present except as otherwise provided in chapters 10 and 16.

11.1.3 The provisions of this section apply in conjunction with chapter 3.

11.1.4 For the purposes of fire fighting, any open deck areas above cofferdams, ballast or void spaces at the after end of the aftermost hold space or at the forward end of the forwardmost hold space should be included in the cargo area.

11.2 Fire water main equipment

11.2.1 All ships, irrespective of size, carrying products which are subject to this Code should comply with the requirements of regulations II-2/4 and II-2/7 of the 1983 SOLAS amendments, except that the required fire pump capacity and fire main and water service pipe diameter should not be limited by the provisions of regulations 4.2.1 and 4.4.1 when the fire pump and fire main are used as part of the water-spray system as permitted by 11.3.3. In addition, the requirements of regulation 4.4.2 should be met at a pressure of at least 5.0 bar gauge.

11.2.2 The arrangements should be such that at least two jets of water can reach any part of the deck in the cargo area and those portions of the cargo containment system and tank covers above the deck. The necessary number of fire hydrants should be located to satisfy the above arrangements and to comply with the requirements of regulations II-2/4.5.1 and II-2/4.8 of the 1983 SOLAS amendments, with hose lengths not exceeding 33 m.

11.2.3 Stop valves should be fitted in any crossover provided and in the fire main or mains at the poop front and at intervals of not more than 40 m between hydrants on the deck in the cargo area for the purpose of isolating damaged sections of the main.

11.2.4 All water nozzles provided for fire-fighting use should be of an approved dual-purpose type capable of producing either a spray or a jet. All pipes, valves nozzles and other fittings in the fire-fighting systems should be resistant to corrosion by seawater, for which purpose galvanized pipe, for example, may be used, and to the effect of fire.

11.2.5 Where the ship's engine-room is unattended, arrangements should be made to start and connect to the fire main at least one fire pump by remote control from the navigating bridge or other control station outside the cargo area.

11.3 Water-spray system

11.3.1 On ships carrying flammable or toxic products or both, a water-spray system for cooling, fire prevention and crew protection should be installed to cover:

.1   exposed cargo tank domes and any exposed parts of cargo tanks;

.2   exposed on-deck storage vessels for flammable or toxic products;

.3   cargo liquid and vapour discharge and loading manifolds and the area of their control valves and any other areas where essential control valves are situated and which should be at least equal to the area of the drip trays provided; and

.4   boundaries of superstructures and deckhouses normally manned, cargo compressor rooms, cargo pump-rooms, store-rooms containing high fire risk items and cargo control rooms, all facing the cargo area. Boundaries of unmanned forecastle structures not containing high fire risk items or equipment do not require water-spray protection.

11.3.2 The system should be capable of covering all areas mentioned in 11.3.1 with a uniformly distributed water-spray of at least $10l/m^2$ per minute for horizontal projected surfaces and $4l/m^2$ per minute for vertical surfaces. For structures having no clearly defined horizontal or vertical surfaces, the capacity of the water-spray system should be the greater of the following:

.1   projected horizontal surface multiplied by 10l/m² per minute; or

.2   actual surface multiplied by 4l/m² per minute.

On vertical surfaces, spacing of nozzles protecting lower areas may take account of anticipated rundown from higher areas. Stop valves should be fitted at intervals in the spray main for the purpose of isolating damaged sections. Alternatively, the system may be divided into two or more sections which may be operated independently provided the necessary controls are located together, aft of the cargo area. A section protecting any area included in 11.3.1.1 and .2 should cover the whole of the athwartship tank grouping which includes that area.

11.3.3 The capacity of the water-spray pumps should be sufficient to deliver the required amount of water to all areas simultaneously or where the system is divided into sections, the arrangements and capacity should be such as to supply water simultaneously to any one section and to the surfaces specified in 11.3.1.3 and .4. Alternatively, the main fire pumps may be used for this service provided that their total capacity is increased by the amount needed for the spray system. In either case, a connection, through a stop valve, should be made between the fire main and water-spray main outside the cargo area.

11.3.4 Subject to the approval of the Administration, water pumps normally used for other services may be arranged to supply the water-spray main.

11.3.5 All pipes, valves, nozzles and other fittings in the water-spray systems should be resistant to corrosion by seawater, for which purpose galvanized pipe, for example, may be used, and to the effect of fire.

11.3.6 Remote starting of pumps supplying the water spray system and remote operation of any normally closed valves in the system should be arranged in suitable locations outside the cargo area, adjacent to the accommodation spaces and readily accessible and operable in the event of fire in the areas protected.

11.4 Dry chemical powder fire-extinguishing systems

11.4.1 Ships in which the carriage of flammable products is intended should be fitted with fixed dry chemical powder type extinguishing systems for the purpose of fighting fire on the deck in the cargo area and bow or stern cargo handling areas if applicable. The system and the dry chemical powder should be adequate for this purpose and satisfactory to the Administration.

11.4.2 The system should be capable of delivering powder from at least two hand hose lines or combination monitor/hand hose lines to any part of the above-deck exposed cargo area including above-deck product piping.

The system should be activated by an inert gas such as nitrogen, used exclusively for this purpose and stored in pressure vessels adjacent to the powder containers.

11.4.3 The system for use in the cargo area should consist of at least two independent self-contained dry chemical powder units with associated controls, pressurizing medium fixed piping, monitors or hand hose lines. For ships with a cargo capacity of less than 1,000 m³ only one such unit need be fitted, subject to approval by the Administration. A monitor should be provided and so arranged as to protect the cargo loading and discharge manifold areas and be capable of actuation and discharge locally and remotely. The monitor is not required to be remotely aimed if it can deliver the necessary powder to all required areas of coverage from a single position. All hand hose lines and monitors should be capable of actuation at the hose storage reel or monitor. At least one hand hose line or monitor should be situated at the after end of the cargo area.

11.4.4 A fire-extinguishing unit having two or more monitors, hand hose lines, or combinations thereof, should have independent pipes with a manifold at the powder container, unless a suitable alternative means is provided to ensure proper performance as approved by the Administration. Where two or more pipes are attached to a unit the arrangement should be such that any or all of the monitors and hand hose lines should be capable of simultaneous or sequential operation at their rated capacities.

11.4.5 The capacity of a monitor should be not less than 10 kg/s. Hand hose lines should be non-kinkable and be fitted with a nozzle of on/off operation and discharge at a rate not less than 3.5 kg/s. The maximum discharge rate should be such as to allow operation by one man. The length of a hand hose line should not exceed 33 m. Where fixed piping is provided between the powder container and a hand hose line or monitor, the length of piping should not exceed that length which is capable of maintaining the powder in a fluidized state during sustained or intermittent use, and which can be purged of powder when the system is shut down. Hand hose lines and nozzles should be of weather-resistant construction or stored in weather-resistant housing or covers and be readily accessible.

11.4.6 A sufficient quantity of dry chemical powder should be stored in each container to provide a minimum 45 s discharge time for all monitors and hand hose lines attached to each powder unit. Coverage from fixed monitors should be in accordance with the following requirements:

Capacity of fixed monitors (kg/s) each:	10	25	45
Maximum distance of coverage (m):	10	30	40

Hand hose lines should be considered to have a maximum effective distance of coverage equal to the length of hose. Special consideration should be given where areas to be protected are substantially higher than the monitor or hand hose reel locations.

11.4.7 Ships fitted with low bow or stern loading and discharge arrangements should be provided with an additional dry chemical powder unit complete with at least one monitor and one hand hose line complying with the requirements of 11.4.1 to 11.4.6. This additional unit should be located to protect the bow or stern loading and discharge arrangements. The area of the cargo line forward or aft of the cargo area should be protected by hand hose lines.

11.5 Cargo compressor and pump-rooms

11.5.1 The cargo compressor and pump-rooms of any ship should be provided with a carbon dioxide system as specified in regulation II-2/5.1 and .2 of the 1974 SOLAS Convention, as amended. A notice should be exhibited at the controls stating that the system is only to be used for fire extinguishing and not for inerting purposes, due to the electrostatic ignition hazard. The alarms referred to in regulation II-2/5.1.6 of the 1983 SOLAS amendments should be safe for use in a flammable cargo vapour–air mixture. For the purpose of this requirement, an extinguishing system should be provided which would be suitable for machinery spaces. However, the amount of carbon dioxide gas carried should be sufficient to provide a quantity of free gas equal to 45% of the gross volume of the cargo compressor and pump-rooms in all cases.

11.5.2 Cargo compressor and pump-rooms of ships which are dedicated to the carriage of a restricted number of cargoes should be protected by an appropriate fire extinguishing system approved by the Administration.

11.6 Firemen's outfits

11.6.1 Every ship carrying flammable products should carry firemen's outfits complying with the requirements of regulation II-2/17 of the 1983 SOLAS amendments as follows:

Total cargo capacity	Number of outfits
5,000 m^3 and below	4
above 5,000 m^3	5

11.6.2 Additional requirements for safety equipment are given in chapter 14.

11.6.3 Any breathing apparatus required as part of a fireman's outfit should be a self-contained air-breathing apparatus having a capacity of at least 1,200 *l* of free air.

Chapter 12

Mechanical ventilation in the cargo area

The requirements of this chapter should be substituted for regulation II-2/59.3 of the 1983 SOLAS amendments.

12.1 Spaces required to be entered during normal cargo handling operations

12.1.1 Electric motor rooms, cargo compressor and pump-rooms, other enclosed spaces which contain cargo handling equipment and similar spaces in which cargo handling operations are performed should be fitted with mechanical ventilation systems capable of being controlled from outside such spaces. Provision should be made to ventilate such spaces prior to entering the compartment and operating the equipment and a warning notice requiring the use of such ventilation should be placed outside the compartment.

12.1.2 Mechanical ventilation inlets and outlets should be arranged to ensure sufficient air movement through the space to avoid the accumulation of flammable or toxic vapours and to ensure a safe working environment, but in no case should the ventilation system have a capacity of less than 30 changes of air per hour based upon the total volume of the space. As an exception, gas-safe cargo control rooms may have eight changes of air per hour.

12.1.3 Ventilation systems should be fixed and, if of the negative pressure type, permit extraction from either the upper or the lower parts of the spaces, or from both the upper and lower parts, depending on the density of the vapours of the products carried.

12.1.4 In rooms housing electric motors driving cargo compressors or pumps, spaces except machinery spaces containing inert gas generators, cargo control rooms if considered as gas-safe spaces and other gas-safe spaces with the cargo area, the ventilation should be of the positive pressure type.

12.1.5 In cargo compressor and pump-rooms and in cargo control rooms if considered gas-dangerous, the ventilation should be of the negative pressure type.

12.1.6 Ventilation exhaust ducts from gas-dangerous spaces should discharge upwards in locations at least 10 m in the horizontal direction from ventilation intakes and openings to accommodation spaces, service spaces and control stations and other gas-safe spaces.

12.1.7 Ventilation intakes should be so arranged as to minimize the possibility of re-cycling hazardous vapours from any ventilation discharge opening.

12.1.8 Ventilation ducts from gas-dangerous spaces should not be led through accommodation, service and machinery spaces or control stations, except as allowed in chapter 16.

12.1.9 Electric motors driving fans should be placed outside the ventilation ducts if the carriage of flammable products is intended. Ventilation fans should not produce a source of vapour ignition in either the ventilated space or the ventilation system associated with the space. Ventilation fans and fan ducts, in way of fans only, for gas-dangerous spaces should be of nonsparking construction defined as:

.1 impellers or housing of nonmetallic construction, due regard being paid to the elimination of static electricity;

.2 impellers and housing of nonferrous materials;

.3 impellers and housing of austenitic stainless steel; and

.4 ferrous impellers and housing with not less than 13 mm design tip clearance.

Any combination of an aluminium or magnesium alloy fixed or rotating component and a ferrous fixed or rotating component, regardless of tip clearance, is considered a sparking hazard and should not be used in these places.

12.1.10 Spare parts should be carried for each type of fan on board referred to in this chapter.

12.1.11 Protection screens of not more than 13 mm square mesh should be fitted in outside openings of ventilation ducts.

12.2 Spaces not normally entered

Hold spaces, interbarrier spaces, void spaces, cofferdams, spaces containing cargo piping and other spaces where cargo vapours may accumulate, should be capable of being ventilated to ensure a safe environment when entry into the spaces is necessary. Where a permanent ventilation system is not provided for such spaces, approved means of portable mechanical ventilation should be provided. Where necessary owing to the arrangement of spaces, such as hold spaces and interbarrier spaces, essential ducting for such ventilation should be permanently installed. Fans or blowers should be clear of personnel access openings, and should comply with 12.1.9.

Chapter 13

Instrumentation (gauging, gas detection)

13.1 General

13.1.1 Each cargo tank should be provided with means for indicating level, pressure and temperature of the cargo. Pressure gauges and temperature indicating devices should be installed in the liquid and vapour piping systems, in cargo refrigerating installations and in the inert gas systems as detailed in this chapter.

13.1.2 Where a secondary barrier is required, permanently installed instrumentation should be provided to detect when the primary barrier fails to be liquid-tight at any location or when liquid cargo is in contact with the secondary barrier at any location. This instrumentation should consist of appropriate gas detecting devices according to 13.6. However, the instrumentation need not be capable of locating the area where liquid cargo leaks through the primary barrier or where liquid cargo is in contact with the secondary barrier.

13.1.3 If the loading and unloading of the ship is performed by means of remotely controlled valves and pumps, all controls and indicators associated with a given cargo tank should be concentrated in one control position.

13.1.4 Instruments should be tested to ensure reliability in the working conditions and recalibrated at regular intervals. Test procedures for instruments and the intervals between recalibration should be approved by the Administration.

13.2 Level indicators for cargo tanks

13.2.1 Each cargo tank should be fitted with at least one liquid level gauging device, designed to operate at pressures not less than the MARVS of the cargo tank and at temperatures within the cargo operating temperature range. Where only one liquid level gauge is fitted it should be so arranged that any necessary maintenance can be carried out while the cargo tank is in service.

13.2.2 Cargo tank liquid level gauges may be of the following types subject to any special requirement for particular cargoes shown in column g in the table of chapter 19:

    .1   indirect devices, which determine the amount of cargo by means such as weighing or pipe flow meters;

.2 closed devices, which do not penetrate the cargo tank, such as devices using radioisotopes or ultrasonic devices;

.3 closed devices, which penetrate the cargo tank, but which form part of a closed system and keep the cargo from being released, such as float type systems, electronic probes, magnetic probes and bubble tube indicators. If a closed gauging device is not mounted directly on the tank it should be provided with a shutoff valve located as close as possible to the tank; and

.4 restricted devices, which penetrate the tank and when in use permit a small quantity of cargo vapour or liquid to escape to the atmosphere, such as fixed tube and slip tube gauges. When not in use, the devices should be kept completely closed. The design and installation should ensure that no dangerous escape of cargo can take place when opening the device. Such gauging devices should be so designed that the maximum opening does not exceed 1.5 mm diameter or equivalent area unless the device is provided with an excess flow valve.

13.2.3 Sighting ports with a suitable protective cover and situated above the liquid level with an internal scale may be allowed by the Administration as a secondary means of gauging for cargo tanks having a design vapour pressure not higher than 0.7 bar.

13.2.4 Tubular gauge glasses should not be fitted. Gauge glasses of the robust type as fitted on high-pressure boilers and fitted with excess flow valves may be allowed by the Administration for deck tanks, subject to any provisions of chapter 17.

13.3 Overflow control

13.3.1 Except as provided in 13.3.2, each cargo tank should be fitted with a high liquid level alarm operating independently of other liquid level indicators and giving an audible and visual warning when activated. Another sensor operating independently of the high liquid level alarm should automatically actuate a shutoff valve in a manner which will both avoid excessive liquid pressure in the loading line and prevent the tank from becoming liquid full. The emergency shutdown valve referred to in 5.6.4 may be used for this purpose. If another valve is used for this purpose, the same information as referred to in 5.6.4 should be available on board. During loading, whenever the use of these valves may possibly create a potential excess pressure surge in the loading system, the Administration and the port Administration may agree to alternative arrangements such as limiting the loading rate, etc.

13.3.2 A high liquid level alarm and automatic shutoff of cargo tank filling need not be required when the cargo tank:

.1 is a pressure tank with a volume not more than 200 m³; or

.2   is designed to withstand the maximum possible pressure during the loading operation and such pressure is below that of the start-to-discharge pressure of the cargo tank relief valve.

13.3.3 Electrical circuits, if any, of level alarms should be capable of being tested prior to loading.

13.4 Pressure gauges

13.4.1 The vapour space of each cargo tank should be provided with a pressure gauge which should incorporate an indicator in the control position required by 13.1.3. In addition, a high-pressure alarm and, if vacuum protection is required, a low-pressure alarm, should be provided on the navigating bridge. Maximum and minimum allowable pressures should be marked on the indicators. The alarms should be activated before the set pressures are reached. For cargo tanks fitted with pressure relief valves, which can be set at more than one set pressure in accordance with 8.2.6, high-pressure alarms should be provided for each set pressure.

13.4.2 Each cargo-pump discharge line and each liquid and vapour cargo manifold should be provided with at least one pressure gauge.

13.4.3 Local-reading manifold pressure gauges should be provided to indicate the pressure between stop valves and hose connections to the shore.

13.4.4 Hold spaces and interbarrier spaces without open connection to the atmosphere should be provided with pressure gauges.

13.5 Temperature indicating devices

13.5.1 Each cargo tank should be provided with at least two devices for indicating cargo temperatures, one placed at the bottom of the cargo tank and the second near the top of the tank, below the highest allowable liquid level. The temperature indicating devices should be marked to show the lowest temperature for which the cargo tank has been approved by the Administration.

13.5.2 When a cargo is carried in a cargo containment system with a secondary barrier at a temperature lower than −55°C, temperature indicating devices should be provided within the insulation or on the hull structure adjacent to cargo containment systems. The devices should give readings at regular intervals and, where applicable, audible warning of temperatures approaching the lowest for which the hull steel is suitable.

13.5.3 If cargo is to be carried at temperatures lower than −55°C, the cargo tank boundaries, if appropriate for the design of the cargo containment system, should be fitted with temperature indicating devices as follows:

  .1   A sufficient number of devices to establish that an unsatisfactory temperature gradient does not occur.

  .2   On one tank a number of devices in excess of those required in 13.5.3.1 in order to verify that the initial cool down procedure is satisfactory. These devices may be either temporary or permanent. When a series of similar ships is built, the second and successive ships need not comply with the requirements of this subparagraph.

13.5.4 The number and position of temperature indicating devices should be to the satisfaction of the Administration.

13.6 Gas detection requirements

13.6.1 Gas detection equipment acceptable to the Administration and suitable for the gases to be carried should be provided in accordance with column f in the table of chapter 19.

13.6.2 In every installation, the positions of fixed sampling heads should be determined with due regard to the density of the vapours of the products intended to be carried and the dilution from compartment purging or ventilation.

13.6.3 Pipe runs from sampling heads should not be led through gas-safe spaces except as permitted by 13.6.5.

13.6.4 Audible and visual alarms from the gas detection equipment, if required by this section, should be located on the navigating bridge, in the control position required by 13.1.3, and at the gas detector readout location.

13.6.5 Gas detection equipment may be located in the control position required by 13.1.3, on the navigating bridge or at other suitable locations. When such equipment is located in a gas-safe space the following conditions should be met:

  .1   gas-sampling lines should have shutoff valves or an equivalent arrangement to prevent cross-communication with gas-dangerous spaces; and

  .2   exhaust gas from the detector should be discharged to the atmosphere in a safe location.

13.6.6 Gas detection equipment should be so designed that it may readily be tested. Testing and calibration should be carried out at regular intervals. Suitable equipment and span gas for this purpose should be carried on board. Where practicable, permanent connections for such equipment should be fitted.

13.6.7 A permanently installed system of gas detection and audible and visual alarms should be provided for:

.1   cargo pump-rooms

.2   cargo compressor rooms;

.3   motor rooms for cargo handling machinery;

.4   cargo control rooms unless designated as gas-safe;

.5   other enclosed spaces in the cargo area where vapour may accumulate including hold spaces and interbarrier spaces for independent tanks other than type C;

.6   ventilation hoods and gas ducts where required by chapter 16; and

.7   airlocks.

13.6.8 The gas detection equipment should be capable of sampling and analysing for each sampling head location sequentially at intervals not exceeding 30 minutes, except that in the case of gas detection for the ventilation hoods and gas ducts referred to in 13.6.7.6 sampling should be continuous. Common sampling lines to the detection equipment should not be fitted.

13.6.9 In the case of products which are toxic or both toxic and flammable, the Administration, except when column h in the table of chapter 19 refers to 17.9, may authorize the use of portable equipment for detection of toxic products as an alternative to a permanently installed system, if such equipment is used before personnel enter the spaces listed in 13.6.7 and at 30-minute intervals while they remain therein.

13.6.10 For the spaces listed in 13.6.7, alarms should be activated for flammable products when the vapour concentration reaches 30% of the lower flammable limit.

13.6.11 In the case of flammable products, where cargo containment systems other than independent tanks are used, hold spaces and interbarrier spaces should be provided with a permanently installed gas detection system capable of measuring gas concentrations of 0% to 100% by volume. The detection equipment, equipped with audible and visual alarms, should be capable of monitoring from each sampling head location sequentially at intervals not exceeding 30 minutes. Alarms should be activated when the vapour concentration reaches the equivalent of 30% of the lower flammable limit in air or such other limit as may be approved by the Administration in the light of particular cargo containment arrangements. Common sampling lines to the detection equipment should not be fitted.

13.6.12 In the case of toxic gases, hold spaces and interbarrier spaces should be provided with a permanently installed piping system for obtaining gas samples from the spaces. Gas from these spaces should be sampled and analysed from each sampling head location by means of fixed or portable equipment at intervals not exceeding 4 h and in any event before personnel enter the space and at 30-minute intervals while they remain therein.

13.6.13 Every ship should be provided with at least two sets of portable gas detection equipment acceptable to the Administration and suitable for the products to be carried.

13.6.14 A suitable instrument for the measurement of oxygen levels in inert atmospheres should be provided.

Chapter 14

Personnel protection

14.1 Protective equipment

Suitable protective equipment including eye protection should be provided for protection of crew members engaged in loading and discharging operations, taking into account the character of the products.

14.2 Safety equipment

14.2.1 Sufficient, but not less than two complete sets of safety equipment in addition to the firemen's outfits required by 11.6.1 each permitting personnel to enter and work in a gas-filled space, should be provided.

14.2.2 One complete set of safety equipment should consist of:

.1 one self-contained air-breathing apparatus not using stored oxygen having a capacity of at least 1,200 *l* of free air;

.2 protective clothing, boots, gloves and tight-fitting goggles;

.3 steel-cored rescue line with belt; and

.4 explosion-proof lamp.

14.2.3 An adequate supply of compressed air should be provided and should consist either of:

.1 one set of fully charged spare air bottles for each breathing apparatus required by 14.2.1;

a special air compressor suitable for the supply of high-pressure air of the required purity; and

a charging manifold capable of dealing with sufficient spare breathing apparatus air bottles for the breathing apparatus required by 14.2.1; or

.2 fully charged spare air bottles with a total free air capacity of at least 6,000 *l* for each breathing apparatus required by 14.2.1.

14.2.4 Alternatively, the Administration may accept a low-pressure air line system with hose connection suitable for use with the breathing apparatus required by 14.2.1. This system should provide sufficient high-pressure air capacity to supply, through pressure reduction devices, enough low-pressure air to enable two men to work in a gas-dangerous space for at least 1 h without using the air bottles of the breathing apparatus. Means should be provided for recharging the fixed air bottles and the breathing apparatus air bottles from a special air compressor suitable for the supply of high-pressure air of the required purity.

14.2.5 Protective equipment required in 14.1 and safety equipment required in 14.2.1 should be kept in suitable, clearly marked lockers located in readily accessible places.

14.2.6 The compressed air equipment should be inspected at least once a month by a responsible officer and the inspection recorded in the ship's log-book, and inspected and tested by an expert at least once a year.

14.3 First-aid equipment

14.3.1 A stretcher which is suitable for hoisting an injured person from spaces below deck should be kept in a readily accessible location.

14.3.2* Medical first-aid equipment including oxygen resuscitation equipment and antidotes, if available, for products carried should be provided on board.

14.4 Personnel protection requirements for individual products

14.4.1 Provisions of 14.4 are applicable to ships carrying products for which those paragraphs are listed in column *i* in the table of chapter 19.

14.4.2 Respiratory and eye protection suitable for emergency escape purposes should be provided for every person on board subject to the following:

- **.1.1** filter-type respiratory protection is unacceptable;

- **.1.2** self-contained breathing apparatus should normally have a duration of service of at least 15 minutes;

- **.2** emergency escape respiratory protection should not be used for fire-fighting or cargo handling purposes and should be marked to that effect;

- **.3** two additional sets of the above respiratory and eye protection should be permanently located in the navigating bridge.

---

* Refer to the *Medical First Aid Guide for Use in Accidents Involving Dangerous Goods* (MFAG), which includes the MFAG numbers of products covered by the IGC Code and the emergency procedures to be applied in the event of an incident. MFAG numbers related to products covered by the Code are given in the table of minimum requirements (chapter 19).

14.4.3 Suitably marked decontamination showers and an eyewash should be available on deck in convenient locations. The showers and eyewash should be operable in all ambient conditions.

14.4.4 In ships of a cargo capacity of 2,000 m³ and over, two complete sets of safety equipment should be provided in addition to the equipment required by 11.6.1 and 14.2.1. At least three spare charged air bottles should be provided for each self-contained air-breathing apparatus required in this paragraph.

14.4.5 Personnel should be protected against the effects of a major cargo release by the provision of a space within the accommodation area designed and equipped to the satisfaction of the Administration.

14.4.6 For certain highly dangerous products, cargo control rooms should not be of the gas-safe type only.

Chapter 15

Filling limits for cargo tanks

15.1 General

15.1.1 No cargo tanks should be more than 98% liquid full at the reference temperature, except as permitted by 15.1.3.

15.1.2 The maximum volume to which a cargo tank may be loaded is determined by the following formula:

$$V_L = 0.98V \frac{\rho_R}{\rho_L}$$

where:

V_L = maximum volume to which the tank may be loaded

V = volume of the tank

ρ_R = relative density of cargo at the reference temperature

ρ_L = relative density of cargo at the loading temperature and pressure.

15.1.3 The Administration may allow a higher filling limit than the limit of 98% specified in 15.1.1 and 15.1.2 at the reference temperature, taking into account the shape of the tank, arrangements of pressure relief valves, accuracy of level and temperature gauging and the difference between the loading temperature and the temperature corresponding to the vapour pressure of the cargo at the set pressure relief valves, provided the conditions specified in 8.2.17 are maintained.

15.1.4 For the purpose of this chapter only, *reference temperature* means:

.1 the temperature corresponding to the vapour pressure of the cargo at the set pressure of the pressure relief valves when no cargo vapour pressure/temperature control as referred to in chapter 7 is provided.

.2 the temperature of the cargo upon termination of loading, during transportation, or at unloading, whichever is the greatest, when a cargo vapour pressure/temperature control as referred to in chapter 7 is provided. If this reference temperature would result in the cargo tank becoming liquid full before the cargo reaches a temperature corresponding to the vapour pressure of the cargo at the set pressure of the relief valves required in 8.2, an additional pressure relieving system complying with 8.3 should be fitted.

15.2 Information to be provided to the master

The maximum allowable loading limits for each cargo tank should be indicated for each product which may be carried, for each loading temperature which may be applied and for the applicable maximum reference temperature, on a list to be approved by the Administration. Pressures at which the pressure relief valves, including those valves required by 8.3, have been set should also be stated on the list. A copy of the list should be permanently kept on board by the master.

Chapter 16

Use of cargo as fuel

16.1 General

16.1.1 Methane (LNG) is the only cargo whose vapour or boil-off gas may be utilized in machinery spaces of category A and in such spaces may be utilized only in boilers, inert gas generators, combustion engines and gas turbines.

16.1.2 These provisions do not preclude the use of gas fuel for auxiliary services in other locations, provided that such other services and locations should be subject to special consideration by the Administration.

16.2 Arrangement of machinery spaces of category A

16.2.1 Spaces in which gas fuel is utilized should be fitted with a mechanical ventilation system and should be arranged in such a way as to prevent the formation of dead spaces. Such ventilation should be particularly effective in the vicinity of electrical equipment and machinery or of other equipment and machinery which may generate sparks. Such a ventilation system should be separated from those intended for other spaces.

16.2.2 Gas detectors should be fitted in these spaces, particularly in the zones where air circulation is reduced. The gas detection system should comply with the requirements of chapter 13.

16.2.3 Electrical equipment located in the double-wall pipe or duct specified in 16.3.1 should be of the intrinsically safe type.

16.3 Gas fuel supply

16.3.1 Gas fuel piping should not pass through accommodation spaces, services spaces, or control stations. Gas fuel piping may pass through or extend into other spaces provided they fulfil one of the following:

  .1 the gas fuel piping should be a double-wall piping system with the gas fuel contained in the inner pipe. The space between the concentric pipes should be pressurized with inert gas at a pressure greater than the gas fuel pressure. Suitable alarms should be provided to indicate a loss of inert gas pressure between the pipes; or

.2   the gas fuel piping should be installed within a ventilated pipe or duct. The air space between the gas fuel piping and inner wall of this pipe or duct should be equipped with mechanical exhaust ventilation having a capacity of at least 30 air changes per hour. The ventilation system should be arranged to maintain a pressure less than the atmospheric pressure. The fan motors should be placed outside the ventilated pipe or duct. The ventilation outlet should be placed in a position where no flammable gas–air mixture may be ignited. The ventilation should always be in operation when there is gas fuel in the piping. Continuous gas detection should be provided to indicate leaks and to shut down the gas fuel supply to the machinery space in accordance with 16.3.10. The master gas fuel valve required by 16.3.7 should close automatically, if the required air flow is not established and maintained by the exhaust ventilation system.

16.3.2 If a gas leak occurs, the gas fuel supply should not be restored until the leak has been found and repaired. Instructions to this effect should be placed in a prominent position in the machinery spaces.

16.3.3 The double-wall piping systems or the ventilated pipe or duct provided for the gas fuel piping should terminate at the ventilation hood or casing required by 16.3.4.

16.3.4 A ventilation hood or casing should be provided for the areas occupied by flanges, valves, etc., and for the gas fuel piping, at the gas fuel utilization units, such as boilers, diesel engines or gas turbines. If this ventilation hood or casing is not served by the exhaust ventilation fan serving the ventilated pipe or duct as specified in 16.3.1.2, then it should be equipped with an exhaust ventilation system and continuous gas detection should be provided to indicate leaks and to shut down the gas fuel supply to the machinery space in accordance with 16.3.10. The master gas fuel valve required by 16.3.7 should close automatically if the required air flow is not established and maintained by the exhaust ventilation system. The ventilation hood or casing should be installed or mounted to permit the ventilating air to sweep across the gas utilization unit and be exhausted at the top of the ventilation hood or casing.

16.3.5 The ventilation inlet and discharge for the required ventilation systems should be respectively from and to a safe location.

16.3.6 Each gas utilization unit should be provided with a set of three automatic valves. Two of these valves should be in series in the gas fuel pipe to the consuming equipment. The third valve should be in a pipe that vents, to a safe location in the open air, that portion of the gas fuel piping that is between the two valves in series. These valves should be arranged so that failure of the necessary forced draught, loss of flame on boiler burners, abnormal pressure in the gas fuel supply line, or failure of the valve control actuating medium will cause the two gas fuel valves which are in series to close automatically and the vent valve to open automatically. Alternatively, the function of one of the valves in series and the vent valve can be incorporated into one valve body so arranged that, when one of the above conditions occurs, flow to the gas utilization unit will be blocked and the vent opened. The three shut-off valves should be arranged for manual reset.

16.3.7 A master gas fuel valve that can be closed from within the machinery space should be provided within the cargo area. The valve should be arranged so as to close automatically if leakage of gas is detected, or loss of ventilation for the duct or casing or loss of pressurization of the double-wall gas fuel piping occurs.

16.3.8 Gas fuel piping in machinery spaces should comply with sections 5.2 to 5.5 as far as found applicable. The piping should, as far as practicable, have welded joints. Those parts of the gas fuel piping which are not enclosed in a ventilated pipe or duct according to 16.3.1 and are on the open deck outside the cargo area should have full penetration butt-welded joints and should be fully radiographed.

16.3.9 Provision should be made for inerting and gas-freeing that portion of the gas fuel piping system located in the machinery space.

16.3.10 Gas detection systems provided in accordance with the requirements of 16.3.1 and 16.3.4 should comply with 13.6.2 and 13.6.4 through 13.6.8 as applicable; they should activate the alarm at 30% of the lower flammable limit and shut down the master gas fuel valve referred to in 16.3.7 before the gas concentration reaches 60% of the lower flammable limit.

16.4 Gas make-up plant and related storage tanks

16.4.1 All equipment (heaters, compressors, filters, etc.) for making up the gas for its use as fuel and the related storage tanks should be located in the cargo area in accordance with 3.1.5.4. If the equipment is in an enclosed space, the space should be ventilated according to section 12.1 of the Code and be equipped with a fixed fire-extinguishing system according to section 11.5 and with a gas detection system according to section 13.6, as applicable.

16.4.2 The compressors should be capable of being remotely stopped from a position which is always and easily accessible, and also from the engine-room. In addition, the compressors should be capable of automatically stopping when the suction pressure reaches a certain value depending on the set pressure of the vacuum relief valves of the cargo tanks. The automatic shutdown device of the compressors should have a manual resetting.

Volumetric compressors should be fitted with pressure relief valves discharging into the suction line of the compressor. The size of the pressure relief valves should be determined in such a way that, with the delivery valve kept closed, the maximum pressure does not exceed by more than 10% the maximum working pressure. The requirements of 5.6.1.3 apply to these compressors.

16.4.3 If the heating medium for the gas fuel evaporator or heater is returned to spaces outside the cargo area it should first go through a degassing tank. The degassing tank should be located in the cargo area. Provisions should be made to detect and alarm the presence of gas in the tank. The vent outlet should be in a safe position and fitted with a flame screen.

16.4.4 Piping and pressure vessels in the gas fuel conditioning system should comply with chapter 5.

16.5 Special requirements for main boilers

16.5.1 Each boiler should have a separate uptake.

16.5.2 A system suitable to ensure the forced draught in the boilers should be provided. The particulars of such a system should be to the satisfaction of the Administration.

16.5.3 Combustion chambers of boilers should be of suitable form such as not to present pockets where gas may accumulate.

16.5.4 The burner systems should be of dual type, suitable to burn either oil fuel or gas fuel alone or oil and gas fuel simultaneously. Only oil fuel should be used during manoeuvring and port operations unless automatic transfer from gas to oil burning is provided, in which case the burning of a combination of oil and gas or gas alone may be permitted provided the system is demonstrated to the satisfaction of the Administration. It should be possible to change over easily and quickly from gas fuel operation to oil fuel operation. Gas nozzles should be fitted in such a way that gas fuel is ignited by the flame of the oil fuel burner. A flame scanner should be installed and arranged to ensure that gas flow to the burner is cut off unless satisfactory ignition has been established and maintained. On the pipe of each gas burner a manually operated shutoff valve should be fitted. An installation should be provided for purging the gas supply piping to the burners by means of inert gas or steam, after the extinguishing of these burners.

16.5.5 Alarm devices should be fitted in order to monitor a possible decrease in liquid fuel oil pressure or a possible failure of the related pumps.

16.5.6 Arrangements should be made that, in case of flame failure of all operating burners for gas or oil or for a combination thereof, the combustion chambers of the boilers are automatically purged before relighting. Arrangements should also be made to enable the boilers to be manually purged and these arrangements should be to the satisfaction of the Administration.

16.6 Special requirements for gas-fired internal combustion engines and gas-fired turbines

Special provisions for gas-fuelled internal combustion engines and for gas turbines will be considered by the Administration in each case.

Chapter 17

Special requirements

17.1 General

The provisions of this chapter are applicable where reference is made in column i in the table of chapter 19. These are requirements additional to the general requirements of the Code.

17.2 Materials of construction

Materials which may be exposed to cargo during normal operations should be resistant to the corrosive action of the gases. In addition, the following materials of construction for cargo tanks, and associated pipelines, valves, fittings and other items of equipment should not be used for certain products as specified in column i in the table of chapter 19:

- **.1** mercury, copper and copper-bearing alloys, and zinc;
- **.2** copper, silver, mercury, magnesium and other acetylide-forming metals;
- **.3** aluminium and aluminium-bearing alloys;
- **.4** copper, copper alloys, zinc and galvanized steel;
- **.5** aluminium, copper and alloys of either;
- **.6** copper and copper-bearing alloys with greater than 1% copper.

17.3 Independent tanks

17.3.1 Products should be carried in independent tanks only.

17.3.2 Products should be carried in type C independent tanks and the provisions of 7.1.3 apply. The design pressure of the cargo tank should take into account any padding pressure or vapour discharge unloading pressure.

17.4 Refrigeration systems

17.4.1 Only the indirect system described in 7.2.4.2 should be used.

17.4.2 For a ship engaged in the carriage of products which readily form dangerous peroxides, recondensed cargo should not be allowed to form stagnant pockets of uninhibited liquid. This may be achieved either by:

.1 using the indirect system described in 7.2.4.2 with the condenser inside the cargo tank; or

.2 using the direct system or combined system described in 7.2.4.1 and .3 respectively, or the indirect system described in 7.2.4.2 with the condenser outside the cargo tank, and designing the condensate system to avoid any places in which liquid could collect and be retained. Where this is impossible inhibited liquid should be added upstream of such a place.

17.4.3 If the ship is to carry consecutively products as specified in 17.4.2 with a ballast passage between, all uninhibited liquid should be removed prior to the ballast voyage. If a second cargo is to be carried between such consecutive cargoes, the reliquefaction system should be thoroughly drained and purged before loading the second cargo. Purging should be carried out using either inert gas or vapour from the second cargo, if compatible. Practical steps should be taken to ensure that polymers or peroxides do not accumulate in the cargo system.

17.5 Deck cargo piping

One hundred per cent radiography of all butt-welded joints in cargo piping exceeding 75 mm in diameter is required.

17.6 Exclusion of air from vapour spaces

Air should be removed from the cargo tanks and associated piping before loading and then subsequently excluded by:

.1 introducing inert gas to maintain a positive pressure. Storage or production capacity of the inert gas should be sufficient to meet normal operating requirements and relief valve leakage. The oxygen content of inert gas should at no time be greater than 0.2% by volume; or

.2 control of cargo temperatures such that a positive pressure is maintained at all times.

17.7 Moisture control

For gases which are non-flammable and may become corrosive or react dangerously with water, moisture control should be provided to ensure that cargo tanks are dry before loading and that during discharge, dry air or cargo vapour is introduced to prevent negative pressures. For the purposes of this paragraph, dry air is air which has a dewpoint of −45°C or below at atmospheric pressure.

17.8 Inhibition

Care should be taken to ensure that the cargo is sufficiently inhibited to prevent polymerization at all times during the voyage. Ships should be provided with a certificate from the manufacturer stating:

.1 name and amount of inhibitor added;

.2 date inhibitor was added and the normally expected duration of its effectiveness;

.3 any temperature limitations affecting the inhibitor;

.4 the action to be taken should the length of the voyage exceed the effective lifetime of the inhibitors.

17.9 Permanently installed toxic gas detectors

17.9.1 Gas sampling lines should not be led into or through gas-safe spaces. Alarms referred to in 13.6.7 should be activated when the vapour concentration reaches the threshold limiting value.

17.9.2 The alternative of using portable equipment in accordance with 13.6.9 should not be permitted.

17.10 Flame screens on vent outlets

Cargo tank vent outlets should be provided with readily renewable and effective flame screens or safety heads of an approved type when carrying a cargo referenced to this section. Due attention should be paid in the design of flame screens and vent heads to the possibility of the blockage of these devices by the freezing of cargo vapour or by icing up in adverse weather conditions. Ordinary protection screens should be fitted after removal of the flame screens.

17.11 Maximum allowable quantity of cargo per tank

When carrying a cargo referenced to this section, the quantity of the cargo should not exceed 3,000 m^3 in any one tank.

17.12 Submerged electric cargo pumps

The vapour space of cargo tanks equipped with submerged electric motor pumps should be inerted to a positive pressure prior to loading, during carriage and during unloading of flammable liquids.

17.13 Ammonia

17.13.1 Anhydrous ammonia may cause stress corrosion cracking in containment and process systems made of carbon-manganese steel or nickel steel. To minimize the risk of this occurring, measures detailed in 17.13.2 to 17.13.8 should be taken, as appropriate.

17.13.2 Where carbon-manganese steel is used, cargo tanks, process pressure vessels and cargo piping should be made of fine-grained steel with a specified minimum yield strength not exceeding 355 N/mm^2 and with an actual yield strength not exceeding 440 N/mm^2. One of the following constructional or operational measures should also be taken:

.1 lower strength material with a specified minimum tensile strength not exceeding 410 N/mm^2 should be used; or

.2 cargo tanks, etc., should be post-weld stress relief heat treated; or

.3 carriage temperature should be maintained preferably at a temperature close to the product's boiling point of $-33°C$ but in no case at a temperature above $-20°C$; or

.4 the ammonia should contain not less than 0.1% w/w water.

17.13.3 If carbon-manganese steels with higher yield properties are used other than those specified in 17.13.2, the completed cargo tanks, piping, etc., should be given a post-weld stress relief heat treatment.

17.13.4 Process pressure vessels and piping of the condensate part of the refrigeration system should be given a post-weld stress relief heat treatment when made of materials mentioned in 17.13.1.

17.13.5 The tensile and yield properties of the welding consumables should exceed those of the tank or piping material by the smallest practical amount.

17.13.6 Nickel steel containing more than 5% nickel and carbon-manganese steel not complying with the requirements of 17.13.2 and 17.13.3 are particularly susceptible to ammonia stress corrosion cracking and should not be used in containment and piping systems for the carriage of this product.

17.13.7 Nickel steel containing not more than 5% nickel may be used provided the carriage temperature complies with the requirements specified in 17.13.2.3.

17.13.8 In order to minimize the risk of ammonia stress corrosion cracking, it is advisable to keep the dissolved oxygen content below 2.5 ppm w/w. This can best be achieved by reducing the average oxygen content in the tanks prior to the introduction of liquid ammonia to less than the values given as a function of the carriage temperature T in the table below:

T (°C)	O_2 (% v/v)
−30 and below	0.90
−20	0.50
−10	0.28
0	0.16
+10	0.10
+20	0.05
+30	0.03

Oxygen percentages for intermediate temperatures may be obtained by direct interpolation.

17.14 Chlorine

17.14.1 Cargo containment system

17.14.1.1 The capacity of each tank should not exceed 600 m³ and the total capacity of all cargo tanks should not exceed 1,200 m³.

17.14.1.2 The tank design vapour pressure should not be less than 13.5 bar (see also 7.1.3 and 17.3.2).

17.14.1.3 Parts of tanks protruding above the upper deck should be provided with protection against thermal radiation taking into account total engulfment by fire.

17.14.1.4 Each tank should be provided with two pressure relief valves. A bursting disc of appropriate material should be installed between the tank and the pressure relief valves. The rupture pressure of the bursting disc should be 1 bar lower than the opening pressure of the pressure relief valve, which should be set at the design vapour pressure of the tank but not less than 13.5 bar gauge. The space between the bursting disc and the relief valve should be connected through an excess flow valve to a pressure gauge and a gas detection system. Provision should be made to keep this space at or near the atmospheric pressure during normal operation.

17.14.1.5 Outlets from pressure relief valves should be arranged in such a way as to minimize the hazards on board the ship as well as to the environment. Leakage from the relief valves should be led through the absorption plant to reduce the gas concentration as far as possible. The relief valve exhaust line should be arranged at the forward end of the ship to discharge outboard at deck level with an arrangement to select either port or starboard side, with a mechanical interlock to ensure that one line is always open.

17.14.1.6 The Administration and the port Administration may require that chlorine is carried in refrigerated state at a specified maximum pressure.

17.14.2 *Cargo piping systems*

17.14.2.1 Cargo discharge should be performed by means of compressed chlorine vapour from shore, dry air or another acceptable gas or fully submerged pumps. The pressure in the vapour space of the tank during discharging should not exceed 10.5 bar gauge. Cargo discharge compressors on board ships should not be accepted by the Administration.

17.14.2.2 The design pressure of the cargo piping system should be not less than 21 bar gauge. The internal diameter of the cargo pipes should not exceed 100 mm. Only pipe bends should be accepted for compensation of pipeline thermal movement. The use of flanged joints should be restricted to a minimum, and when used the flanges should be of the welding neck type with tongue and groove.

17.14.2.3 Relief valves of the cargo piping system should discharge to the absorption plant (see also 8.2.16).

17.14.3 *Materials*

17.14.3.1 The cargo tanks and cargo piping systems should be made of steel suitable for the cargo and for a temperature of −40°C, even if a higher transport temperature is intended to be used.

17.14.3.2 The tanks should be thermally stress relieved. Mechanical stress relief should not be accepted as an equivalent.

17.14.4 *Instrumentation – safety devices*

17.14.4.1 The ship should be provided with a chlorine absorbing plant with connections to the cargo piping system and the cargo tanks. The absorbing plant should be capable of neutralizing at least 2% of the total cargo capacity at a reasonable absorption rate.

17.14.4.2 During the gas-freeing of cargo tanks, vapours should not be discharged to the atmosphere.

17.14.4.3 A gas detecting system should be provided capable of monitoring chlorine concentrations of at least 1 ppm by volume. Suction points should be located:

.1 near the bottom of the hold spaces;

.2 in the pipes from the safety relief valves;

    .3   at the outlet from the gas absorbing plant;

    .4   at the inlet to the ventilation systems for the accommodation, service and machinery spaces and control stations;

    .5   on deck at the forward end, in the middle and at the after end of the cargo area. (Only required to be used during cargo handling and gas-freeing operations.)

The gas detection system should be provided with an audible and visual alarm with a set point of 5 ppm.

17.14.4.4 Each cargo tank should be fitted with a high-pressure alarm giving an audible alarm at a pressure equal to 10.5 bar gauge.

17.14.5 *Personnel protection*

In addition to the requirements given in chapter 14 the following requirements should be met:

    .1   The enclosed space required by 14.4.5 should be easily and quickly accessible from the open deck and from accommodation spaces and should be capable of being rapidly closed gastight. Access to this space from the deck and from the accommodation spaces should be by means of an airlock. The space should be so designed as to accommodate the entire crew of the ship and be provided with a source of uncontaminated air for a period of not less than 4 h. One of the decontamination showers required by 14.4.3 should be located near the air-lock to the space.

    .2   A compressor and the necessary equipment for filling the air bottles should be provided.

    .3   One set of oxygen therapy equipment should be carried in the space referred to in 17.14.5.1.

17.14.6 *Filling limits for cargo tanks*

17.14.6.1 The requirements of 15.1.4.2 do not apply when it is intended to carry chlorine.

17.14.6.2 The chlorine content of the gas in the vapour space of the cargo tank after loading should be greater than 80% by volume.

17.15 Diethyl ether and vinyl ethyl ether

17.15.1 The cargo should be discharged only by deepwell pumps or by hydraulically operated submerged pumps. These pumps should be of a type designed to avoid liquid pressure against the shaft gland.

17.15.2 Inert gas displacement may be used for discharging cargo from type C independent tanks provided the cargo system is designed for the expected pressure.

17.16 Ethylene oxide

17.16.1 For the carriage of ethylene oxide the requirements of 17.20 apply, with the additions and modifications as given in this section.

17.16.2 Deck tanks should not be used for the carriage of ethylene oxide.

17.16.3 Stainless steels types 416 and 442 as well as cast iron should not be used in ethylene oxide cargo containment and piping systems.

17.16.4 Before loading, tanks should be thoroughly and effectively cleaned to remove all traces of previous cargoes from tanks and associated pipework, except where the immediate prior cargo has been ethylene oxide, propylene oxide or mixtures of these products. Particular care should be taken in the case of ammonia in tanks made of steel other than stainless steel.

17.16.5 Ethylene oxide should be discharged only by deepwell pumps or inert gas displacement. The arrangement of pumps should comply with 17.20.5.3.

17.16.6 Ethylene oxide should be carried refrigerated only and maintained at temperatures of less than 30°C.

17.16.7 Pressure relief valves should be set at a pressure of not less than 5.5 bar gauge. The maximum set pressure should be specially approved by the Administration.

17.16.8 The protective padding of nitrogen gas as required by 17.20.15 should be such that the nitrogen concentration in the vapour space of the cargo tank will at no time be less than 45% by volume.

17.16.9 Before loading and at all times when the cargo tank contains ethylene oxide liquid or vapour, the cargo tank should be inerted with nitrogen.

17.16.10 The water-spray system required by paragraph 17.20.17 and that required by 11.3 should operate automatically in a fire involving the cargo containment system.

17.16.11 A jettisoning arrangement should be provided to allow the emergency discharge of ethylene oxide in the event of uncontrollable self-reaction.

17.17 Isopropylamine and monoethylamine

Separate piping systems should be provided as defined in 1.3.32.

17.18 Methyl acetylene-propadiene mixtures

17.18.1 Methyl acetylene-propadiene mixtures should be suitably stabilized for transport. Additionally, upper limits of temperature and pressure during the refrigeration should be specified for the mixtures.

17.18.2 Examples of acceptable, stabilized compositions are:

  .1 *Composition 1*

  .1.1 maximum methyl acetylene to propadiene molar ratio of 3 to 1;

  .1.2 maximum combined concentration of methyl acetylene and propadiene of 65 mol per cent;

  .1.3 minimum combined concentration of propane, butane, and isobutane of 24 mol per cent, of which at least one third (on a molar basis) must be butanes and one third propane; and

  .1.4 maximum combined concentration of propylene and butadiene of 10 mol per cent.

  .2 *Composition 2*

  .2.1 maximum methyl acetylene and propadiene combined concentration of 30 mol per cent;

  .2.2 maximum methyl acetylene concentration of 20 mol per cent;

  .2.3 maximum propadiene concentration of 20 mol per cent;

  .2.4 maximum propylene concentration of 45 mol per cent;

  .2.5 maximum butadiene and butylenes combined concentration of 2 mol per cent;

  .2.6 minimum saturated C_4 hydrocarbon concentration of 4 mol per cent; and

  .2.7 minimum propane concentration of 25 mol per cent.

17.18.3 Other compositions may be accepted provided the stability of the mixture is demonstrated to the satisfaction of the Administration.

17.18.4 A ship carrying methyl acetylene-propadiene mixtures should preferably have an indirect refrigeration system as required in 7.2.4.2. Alternatively, a ship not provided with indirect refrigeration may utilize direct vapour compression refrigeration subject to pressure and temperature limitations depending on the composition. For the example compositions given in 17.18.2, the following features should be provided:

.1 A vapour compressor that does not raise the temperature and pressure of the vapour above 60°C and 17.5 bar gauge during its operation, and that does not allow vapour to stagnate in the compressor while it continues to run.

.2 Discharge piping from each compressor stage or each cylinder in the same stage of a reciprocating compressor should have:

.2.1 two temperature-actuated shutdown switches set to operate at 60°C or less;

.2.2 a pressure-actuated shutdown switch set to operate at 17.5 bar gauge or less; and

.2.3 a safety relief valve set to relieve at 18.0 bar gauge or less.

.3 The relief valve required by 17.18.4.2.3 should vent to a mast meeting the requirements of 8.2.9, 8.2.10, 8.2.13 and 8.2.14 and should not relieve into the compressor suction line.

.4 An alarm that sounds in the cargo control position and in the navigating bridge when a high-pressure switch, or a high-temperature switch operates.

17.18.5 The piping system, including the cargo refrigeration system, for tanks to be loaded with methyl acetylene-propadiene mixtures should be either independent (as defined in 1.3.20) or separate (as defined in 1.3.32) from piping and refrigeration systems for other tanks. This segregation applies to all liquid and vapour vent lines and any other possible connections, such as common inert gas supply lines.

17.19 Nitrogen

Materials of construction and ancillary equipment such as insulation should be resistant to the effects of high oxygen concentrations caused by condensation and enrichment at the low temperatures attained in parts of the cargo system. Due consideration should be given to ventilation in such areas where condensation might occur to avoid the stratification of oxygen-enriched atmosphere.

17.20 Propylene oxide and mixtures of ethylene oxide-propylene oxide with ethylene oxide content of not more than 30% by weight

17.20.1 Products transported under the provisions of this section should be acetylene-free.

17.20.2.1 Unless cargo tanks are properly cleaned, these products should not be carried in tanks which have contained as one of the three previous cargoes any product known to catalyse polymerization, such as:

.1 anhydrous ammonia and ammonia solutions;

.2 amines and amine solutions;

.3 oxidizing substances (e.g. chlorine).

17.20.2.2 Before loading, tanks should be thoroughly and effectively cleaned to remove all traces of previous cargoes from tanks and associated pipework, except where the immediate prior cargo has been propylene oxide or ethylene oxide-propylene oxide mixtures. Particular care should be taken in the case of ammonia in tanks made of steel other than stainless steel.

17.20.2.3 In all cases, the effectiveness of cleaning procedures for tanks and associated pipework should be checked by suitable testing or inspection to ascertain that no traces of acidic or alkaline materials remain that might create a hazardous situation in the presence of these products.

17.20.2.4 Tanks should be entered and inspected prior to each initial loading of these products to ensure freedom from contamination, heavy rust deposits and any visible structural defects. When cargo tanks are in continuous service for these products, such inspections should be performed at intervals of not more than two years.

17.20.2.5 Tanks for the carriage of these products should be of steel or stainless steel construction.

17.20.2.6 Tanks which have contained these products may be used for other cargoes after thorough cleaning of tanks and associated pipework systems by washing or purging.

17.20.3.1 All valves, flanges, fittings and accessory equipment should be of a type suitable for use with these products and should be constructed of steel or stainless steel or other material acceptable to the Administration. The chemical composition of all material used should be submitted to the Administration for approval prior to fabrication. Discs or disc faces, seats and other wearing parts of valves should be made of stainless steel containing not less than 11% chromium.

17.20.3.2 Gaskets should be constructed of materials which do not react with, dissolve in, or lower the autoignition temperature of these products and which are fire-resistant and possess adequate mechanical behaviour. The surface presented to the cargo should be polytetrafluoroethylene (PTFE) or materials giving a similar degree of safety by their inertness. Spirally-wound stainless steel with a filler of PTFE or similar fluorinated polymer may be accepted by the Administration.

17.20.3.3 Insulation and packing if used should be of a material which does not react with, dissolve in, or lower the autoignition temperature of these products.

17.20.3.4 The following materials are generally found unsatisfactory for gaskets, packing and similar uses in containment systems for these products and would require testing before being approved by the Administration:

    .1   Neoprene or natural rubber if it comes into contact with the products;

    .2   Asbestos or binders used with asbestos;

    .3   Materials containing oxides of magnesium, such as mineral wools.

17.20.4 Filling and discharge piping should extend to within 100 mm of the bottom of the tank or any sump.

17.20.5.1 The products should be loaded and discharged in such a manner that venting of the tanks to atmosphere does not occur. If vapour return to shore is used during tank loading, the vapour return system connected to a containment system for the product should be independent of all other containment systems.

17.20.5.2 During discharging operations, the pressure in the cargo tank should be maintained above 0.07 bar gauge.

17.20.5.3 The cargo should be discharged only by deepwell pumps, hydraulically operated submerged pumps, or inert gas displacement. Each cargo pump should be arranged to ensure that the product does not heat significantly if the discharge line from the pump is shut off or otherwise blocked.

17.20.6 Tanks carrying these products should be vented independently of tanks carrying other products. Facilities should be provided for sampling the tank contents without opening the tank to atmosphere.

17.20.7 Cargo hoses used for transfer of these products should be marked "FOR ALKYLENE OXIDE TRANSFER ONLY".

17.20.8 Hold spaces should be monitored for these products. Hold spaces surrounding type A and B independent tanks should also be inerted and monitored for oxygen. The oxygen content of these spaces should be maintained below 2%. Portable sampling equipment is satisfactory.

17.20.9 Prior to disconnecting shore-lines, the pressure in liquid and vapour lines should be relieved through suitable valves installed at the loading header. Liquid and vapour from these lines should not be discharged to atmosphere.

17.20.10 Tanks should be designed for the maximum pressure expected to be encountered during loading, carriage or unloading of cargo.

17.20.11 Tanks for the carriage of propylene oxide with a design vapour pressure of less than 0.6 bar and tanks for the carriage of ethylene oxide-propylene oxide mixtures with a design vapour pressure of less than 1.2 bar should have a cooling system to maintain the cargo below the reference temperature. For reference temperature see 15.1.4.1.

17.20.12 Pressure relief valve settings should not be less than 0.2 bar gauge and for type C independent cargo tanks not greater than 7.0 bar gauge for the carriage of propylene oxide and not greater than 5.3 bar gauge for the carriage of ethylene oxide-propylene oxide mixtures.

17.20.13.1 The piping system for tanks to be loaded with these products should be completely separate from piping systems for all other tanks, including empty tanks, and from all cargo compressors. If the piping system for the tanks to be loaded with these products is not independent as defined in 1.3.20 the required piping separation should be accomplished by the removal of spool pieces, valves, or other pipe sections and the installation of blank flanges at these locations. The required separation applies to all liquid and vapour piping, liquid and vapour vent lines and any other possible connections such as common inert gas supply lines.

17.20.13.2 The products should be transported only in accordance with cargo handling plans that have been approved by the Administration. Each intended loading arrangement should be shown on a separate cargo-handling plan. Cargo handling plans should show the entire cargo piping system and the locations for installation of blank flanges needed to meet the above piping separation requirements. A copy of each approved cargo handling plan should be kept on board the ship. The International Certificate of Fitness for the Carriage of Liquefied Gases in Bulk should be endorsed to include reference to the approved cargo handling plans.

17.20.13.3 Before each initial loading of these products and before every subsequent return to such service, certification verifying that the required piping separation has been achieved should be obtained from a responsible person acceptable to the port Administration and carried on board the ship. Each connection between a blank flange and pipeline flange should be fitted with a wire and seal by the responsible person to ensure that inadvertent removal of the blank flange is impossible.

17.20.14 The maximum allowable tank filling limits for each tank should be indicated for each loading temperature which may be applied and for the applicable maximum reference temperature, on a list to be approved by the Administration. A copy of the list should be permanently kept on board by the master.

17.20.15 The cargo should be carried under a suitable protective padding of nitrogen gas. An automatic nitrogen make-up system should be installed to prevent the tank pressure falling below 0.07 bar gauge in the event of

144

product temperature fall due to ambient conditions or malfunctioning of refrigeration system. Sufficient nitrogen should be available on board to satisfy the demand of the automatic pressure control. Nitrogen of commercially pure quality (99.9% by volume) should be used for padding. A battery of nitrogen bottles connected to the cargo tanks through a pressure reduction valve satisfies the intention of the expression "automatic" in this context.

17.20.16 The cargo tank vapour space should be tested prior to and after loading to ensure that the oxygen content is 2% by volume or less.

17.20.17 A water-spray system of sufficient capacity should be provided to blanket effectively the area surrounding the loading manifold, the exposed deck piping associated with product handling and the tank domes. The arrangement of piping and nozzles should be such as to give a uniform distribution rate of 10 l/m^2 per minute. The water-spray system should be capable of both local and remote manual operation and the arrangement should ensure that any spilled cargo is washed away. Remote manual operation should be arranged such that remote starting of pumps supplying the water-spray system and remote operation of any normally closed valves in the system can be carried out from a suitable location outside the cargo area, adjacent to the accommodation spaces and readily accessible and operable in the event of fire in the areas protected. Additionally, a water hose with pressure to the nozzle, when ambient temperatures permit, should be connected ready for immediate use during loading and unloading operations.

17.21 Vinyl chloride

In cases where polymerization of vinyl chloride is prevented by addition of an inhibitor, 17.8 is applicable. In cases where no or insufficient inhibitor has been added, any inert gas used for the purposes of 17.6 should contain not more oxygen than 0.1%. Before loading is started, inert gas samples from the tanks and piping should be analysed. When vinyl chloride is carried, a positive pressure should always be maintained in the tanks, also during ballast voyages between successive carriages.

Chapter 18

Operating requirements

18.1 Cargo information

18.1.1 Information should be on board and available to all concerned, giving the necessary data for the safe carriage of cargo. Such information should include for each product carried:

.1 a full description of the physical and chemical properties necessary for the safe containment of the cargo;

.2 action to be taken in the event of spills or leaks;

.3 counter-measures against accidental personal contact;

.4 fire-fighting procedures and fire-fighting media;

.5 procedures for cargo transfer, gas-freeing, ballasting, tank cleaning and changing cargoes;

.6 special equipment needed for the safe handling of the particular cargo;

.7 minimum allowable inner hull steel temperatures; and

.8 emergency procedures.

18.1.2 Products required to be inhibited should be refused if the certificate required by 17.8 is not supplied.

18.1.3 A copy of this Code or national regulations incorporating the provisions of this Code should be on board every ship covered by this Code.

18.2 Compatibility

18.2.1 The master should ascertain that the quantity and characteristics of each product to be loaded are within the limits indicated in the International Certificate of Fitness for the Carriage of Liquefied Gases in Bulk provided for in 1.5 and in the Loading and Stability Information booklet provided for in 2.2.5 and that products are listed in the International Certificate of Fitness for the Carriage of Liquefied Gases in Bulk as required under section 3 of the Certificate.

18.2.2 Care should be taken to avoid dangerous chemical reactions if cargoes are mixed. This is of particular significance in respect of:

.1 tank cleaning procedures required between successive cargoes in the same tank; and

.2   simultaneous carriage of cargoes which react when mixed. This should be permitted only if the complete cargo systems including, but not limited to, cargo pipework, tanks, vent systems and refrigeration systems are separated as defined in 1.3.32.

18.3 Personnel training*

18.3.1 Personnel involved in cargo operations should be adequately trained in handling procedures.

18.3.2 All personnel should be adequately trained in the use of protective equipment provided on board and have basic training in the procedures, appropriate to their duties, necessary under emergency conditions.

18.3.3 Officers should be trained in emergency procedures to deal with conditions of leakage, spillage or fire involving the cargo and a sufficient number of them should be instructed and trained in essential first aid for the cargoes carried.

18.4 Entry into spaces

18.4.1 Personnel should not enter cargo tanks, hold spaces, void spaces, cargo-handling spaces or other enclosed spaces where gas may accumulate, unless:

.1   the gas content of the atmosphere in such space is determined by means of fixed or portable equipment to ensure oxygen sufficiency and the absence of toxic atmosphere; or

.2   personnel wear breathing apparatus and other necessary protective equipment and the entire operation is under the close supervision of a responsible officer.

18.4.2 Personnel entering any space designated as gas-dangerous on a ship carrying flammable products should not introduce any potential source of ignition into the space unless it has been certified gas-free and is maintained in that condition.

---

* Refer to the provisions of the International Convention on Standards of Training, Certification and Watchkeeping for Seafarers, 1978, and in particular to the Mandatory minimum requirements for the training and qualifications of masters, officers and ratings of liquefied gas tankers, regulation V/3, chapter V, of the annex to that Convention, and to resolution 12 of the International Conference on Training and Certification of Seafarers, 1978.

18.4.3.1 For internal insulation tanks, special fire precautions should be taken in the event of hot work carried out in the vicinity of the tanks. For this purpose, gas absorbing and de-absorbing characteristics of the insulation material should be taken into account.

18.4.3.2 For internal insulation tanks, repairs should be carried out in accordance with the procedures provided for in paragraph 4.4.7.6.

18.5 Carriage of cargo at low temperature

18.5.1 When carrying cargoes at low temperatures:

    .1   if provided, the heating arrangements associated with cargo containment systems should be operated in such a manner as to ensure that the temperature does not fall below that for which the material of the hull structure is designed;

    .2   loading should be carried out in such a manner as to ensure that unsatisfactory temperature gradients do not occur in any cargo tank, piping or other ancillary equipment; and

    .3   when cooling down tanks from temperatures at or near ambient, the cool-down procedure laid down for that particular tank, piping and ancillary equipment should be followed closely.

18.6 Protective equipment

Personnel should be made aware of the hazards associated with the cargo being handled and should be instructed to act with care and use the appropriate protective equipment as mentioned in 14.1 during cargo handling.

18.7 Systems and controls

Cargo emergency shutdown and alarm systems involved in cargo transfer should be tested and checked before cargo handling operations begin. Essential cargo handling controls should also be tested and checked prior to transfer operations.

18.8 Cargo transfer operations

18.8.1 Transfer operations including emergency procedures should be discussed between ship personnel and the persons responsible at the shore facility prior to commencement and communications maintained throughout the transfer operations.

18.8.2 The closing time of the valve referred to in 13.3.1 (i.e. time from shutdown signal initiation to complete valve closure) should not be greater than:

$$\frac{3600\ U}{LR}\ \text{(s)}$$

where:

U = ullage volume at operating signal level (m³)

LR = maximum loading rate agreed between ship and shore facility (m³/h).

The loading rate should be adjusted to limit surge pressure on valve closure to an acceptable level taking into account the loading hose or arm, the ship and the shore piping systems where relevant.

18.9 Additional operating requirements

Additional operating requirements will be found in the following paragraphs of the Code: 3.8.4, 3.8.5, 7.1.1.5, 8.2.5, 8.2.7, 9.4.2, 12.1.1, 12.1.10, 13.1.4, 14.2.5, 14.2.6, 14.3.1, 15.1, 15.2, 16.2.2, 17.4.2, 17.6, 17.7, 17.12, 17.13, 17.14, 17.15, 17.16, 17.17, 17.18, 17.20.

Chapter 19

Summary of minimum requirements

Explanatory notes to the summary of minimum requirements

UN numbers	The UN numbers as listed in the table of chapter 19 are intended for information only

Vapour detection
required (column f)

F — Flammable vapour detection

T — Toxic vapour detection

O — Oxygen analyser

F + T — Flammable and toxic vapour detection

Gauging – types
permitted (column g)

I — Indirect or closed, as described in 13.2.2.1 and .2

C — Indirect, or closed, as described in 13.2.2.1, .2 and .3

R — Indirect, closed or restricted, as described in 13.2.2.1, .2, .3 and .4

Refrigerant gases

Non-toxic and non-flammable gases such as:

dichlorodifluoromethane (1028)

dichloromonofluoromethane (1029)

dichlorotetrafluoroethane (1958)

monochlorodifluoromethane (1018)

monochlorotetrafluoroethane (1021)

monochlorotrifluoromethane (1022)

Unless otherwise specified, gas mixtures containing less than 5% total acetylenes may be transported with no further requirements than those provided for the major components.

MFAG numbers are provided for information on the emergency procedures to be applied in the event of an incident involving the products covered by the IGC Code. Where any of the products listed are carried at low temperature from which frostbite may occur, MFAG no. 620 is also applicable.

a Product name	b UN number	c Ship type	d Independent tank type C required	e Control of vapour space within cargo tanks	f Vapour detection	g Gauging	h MFAC table no.	i Special requirements
Acetaldehyde	1089	2G/2PG	–	Inert	F+T	C	300	14.4.3, 14.4.4, 17.4.1, 17.6.1
Ammonia, anhydrous	1005	2G/2PG	–	–	T	C	725	14.4.2, 14.4.3, 14.4.4, 17.2.1, 17.13
Butadiene	1010	2G/2PG	–	–	F	R	310	17.2.2, 17.4.2, 17.4.3, 17.6, 17.8
Butane	1011	2G/2PG	–	–	F	R	310	
Butane-propane mixtures	1011/1978	2G/2PG	–	–	F	R	310	
Butylenes	1012	2G/2PG	–	–	F	R	310	
Chlorine	1017	1G	Yes	Dry	T	I	740	14.4, 17.3.2, 17.4.1, 17.5, 17.7, 17.9, 17.14
Diethyl ether*	1155	2G/2PG	–	Inert	F+T	C	330	14.4.2, 14.4.3, 17.2.6, 17.3.1, 17.6.1, 17.10, 17.11, 17.15

* This cargo is also covered by the IBC Code.

151

a Product name	b UN number	c Ship type	d Independent tank type C required	e Control of vapour space within cargo tanks	f Vapour detection	g Gauging	h MFAC table no.	i Special requirements
Dimethylamine	1032	2G/2PG	–	–	F+T	C	320	14.4.2, 14.4.3, 14.4.4, 17.2.1
Ethane	1961	2G	–	–	F	R	310	
Ethyl chloride	1037	2G/2PG	–	–	F+T	R	340	
Ethylene	1038	2G	–	–	F	R	310	
Ethylene oxide	1040	1G	Yes	Inert	F+T	C	365	14.4.2, 14.4.3, 14.4.4, 14.4.6, 17.2.2, 17.3.2, 17.4.1, 17.5, 17.6.1, 17.16
Ethylene oxide-propylene oxide mixtures with ethylene oxide content of not more than 30% by weight*	2983	2G/2PG	–	Inert	F+T	C	365	14.4.3, 17.3.1, 17.4.1, 17.6.1, 17.10, 17.11, 17.20

* This cargo is also covered by the IBC Code.

a Product name	b UN number	c Ship type	d Independent tank type C required	e Control of vapour space within cargo tanks	f Vapour detection	g Gauging	h MFAG table no.	i Special requirements
Isoprene*	1218	2G/2PG	–	–	F	R	310	14.4.3, 17.8, 17.10, 17.12
Isopropylamine*	1221	2G/2PG	–	–	F+T	C	320	14.4.2, 14.4.3, 17.2.4, 17.10, 17.11, 17.12, 17.17
Methane (LNG)	1972	2G	–	–	F	C	620	
Methyl acetylene-propadiene mixtures	1060	2G/2PG	–	–	F	R	310	17.18
Methyl bromide	1062	1G	Yes	–	F+T	C	345	14.4, 17.2.3, 17.3.2, 17.4.1, 17.5, 17.9
Methyl chloride	1063	2G/2PG	–	–	F+T	C	340	17.2.3
Monoethylamine*	1036	2G/2PG	–	–	F+T	C	320	14.4.2, 14.4.3, 14.4.4, 17.2.1, 17.3.1, 17.10, 17.11, 17.12, 17.17
Nitrogen	2040	3G	–	–	O	C	620	17.19

* This cargo is also covered by the IBC Code.

153

a	b	c	d	e	f	g	h	i
Product name	UN number	Ship type	Independent tank type C required	Control of vapour space within cargo tanks	Vapour detection	Gauging	MFAG table no.	Special requirements
Pentanes (all isomers)*	1265	2G/2PG	–	–	F	R	310	14.4.4, 17.10, 17.12
Pentene (all isomers)*	1265	2G/2PG	–	–	F	R	310	14.4.4, 17.10, 17.12
Propane	1978	2G/2PG	–	–	F	R	310	
Propylene	1077	2G/2PG	–	–	F	R	310	
Propylene oxide*	1280	2G/2PG	–	Inert	F + T	C	365	14.4.3, 17.3.1, 17.4.1, 17.6.1, 17.10, 17.11, 17.20
Refrigerant gases (see notes)	–	3G	–	–	–	R	350	
Sulphur dioxide	1079	1G	Yes	Dry	T	C	635	14.4, 17.3.2, 17.4.1, 17.5, 17.7, 17.9
Vinyl chloride	1086	2G/2PG	–	–	F + T	C	340	14.4.2, 14.4.3, 17.2.2, 17.2.3, 17.3.1, 17.6, 17.21

* This cargo is also covered by the IBC Code.

a	b	c	d	e	f	g	h	
Product name	UN number	Ship type	Independent tank type C required	Control of vapour space within cargo tanks	Vapour detection	Gauging	MFAG table no.	Special requirements
Vinyl ethyl ether*	1302	2G/2PG	–	Inert	F+T	C	330	14.4.2, 14.4.3, 17.2.2, 17.3.1, 17.6.1, 17.8, 17.10, 17.11, 17.15
Vinylidene chloride*	1303	2G/2PG	–	Inert	F+T	R	340	14.4.2, 14.4.3, 17.2.5, 17.6.1, 17.8, 17.10, 17.11

---
* This cargo is also covered by the IBC Code.

155

Appendix

**Model form of International Certificate of Fitness
for the Carriage of Liquefied Gases in Bulk**

INTERNATIONAL CERTIFICATE OF FITNESS FOR THE CARRIAGE OF LIQUEFIED GASES IN BULK

(Official seal)

Issued under the provisions of the
INTERNATIONAL CODE FOR THE CONSTRUCTION AND EQUIPMENT
OF SHIPS CARRYING LIQUEFIED GASES IN BULK
(resolution MSC.5(48))

under the authority of the Government of

. . . .
(full official designation of country)

by . . . .
*(full official designation of the competent person or
organization recognized by the Administration)*

Name of ship	Distinctive number or letters	Port of registry	Cargo capacity (m^3)	Ship type (section 2.1 of the Code)[1]

Date on which keel was laid or on which the ship was at a similar stage of construction or (in the case of a converted ship) date on which conversion to a gas carrier was commenced:

. . . .

The Certificate should be drawn up in the official language of the issuing country. If the language used is neither English nor French, the text should include a translation into one of these languages.

The ship also complies fully with the following amendments to the Code:

. . . .

. . . .

The ship is exempted from compliance with the following provisions of the Code:

. . . .

. . . .

THIS IS TO CERTIFY:

1   .1   That the ship has been surveyed in accordance with the provisions of 1.5 of the Code;

   .2   that the survey showed that the structure, equipment, fittings, arrangements and materials of the ship and the conditions thereof are in all respects satisfactory and that the ship complies with the relevant provisions of the Code.

2   That the following design criteria have been used:

   .1   ambient air temperature . . . . $°C^2$

   .2   ambient water temperature . . . . $°C^2$

   .3

Tank type and number	Stress factors[3]				Materials[3]	MARVS
	A	B	C	D		
Cargo piping						

   NB   Tank numbers referred to in this list are identified on attachment 2, signed and dated tank plan.

   .4   Mechanical properties of the cargo tank material were determined at . . . . $°C^4$

3   That the ship is suitable for the carriage in bulk of the following products, provided that all relevant operational provisions of the Code are observed.[5]

Products	Conditions of carriage (tank numbers, etc.)

Continued on attachment 1, additional signed and dated sheets.

Tank numbers referred to in this list are identified on attachment 2, signed and dated tank plan.

4   That in accordance with sections 1.4/2.8.2* the provisions of the Code are modified in respect of the ship in the following manner:

5   That the ship must be loaded:

*.1   in accordance with the loading conditions provided in the approved loading Manual, stamped and dated . . . . and signed by a responsible officer of the Administration, or of an organization recognized by the Administration;

*.2   in accordance with the loading limitations appended to this Certificate.

Where it is required to load the ship other than in accordance with the above instruction, then the necessary calculations to justify the proposed loading conditions should be communicated to the certifying Administration who may authorize in writing the adoption of the proposed loading condition.**

* Delete as appropriate

_____

** Instead of being incorporated in the Certificate, this text may be appended to the Certificate if duly signed and stamped.

This Certificate is valid until . . . .

Issued at . . . .
(Place of issue of Certificate)

. . . . **19** . . . .
(date of issue)   *(signature of authorized official
                                    issuing the Certificate)*

*(seal or stamp of issuing
Authority, as appropriate)*

Notes on completion of Certificate:

[1] *Ship type:* Any entry under this column must be related to all relevant recommendations, e.g. an entry "type 2G" should mean type 2G in all respects prescribed by the Code.

[2] Paragraphs 2.1 and 2.2: The ambient temperatures accepted or required by the Administration for the purposes of 4.8.1 of the Code to be inserted.

[3] Paragraph 2.3: Stress factors and materials as accepted or required by the Administration for the purposes of 4.5.1.4 and 4.5.1.6 of the Code to be inserted.

[4] Paragraph 2.4: Temperature accepted by the Administration for the purposes of 4.5.1.7 to be inserted.

[5] Paragraph 3: Only products listed in chapter 19 of the Code or which have been evaluated by the Administration in accordance with paragraph 1.1.6 of the Code, or their compatible mixtures having physical proportions within the limitations of tank design, should be listed. In respect of the latter "new" products, any special requirements provisionally prescribed should be noted.

ENDORSEMENT FOR MANDATORY ANNUAL SURVEYS

THIS IS TO CERTIFY that at a mandatory annual survey required by 1.5.2.1.4 of the International Code for the Construction and Equipment of Ships Carrying Liquefied Gases in Bulk, the ship was found to comply with the relevant provisions of the Code.

Signed: ....
(signature of authorized official)

Place: ....

Date: ....

(seal or stamp of the Authority, as appropriate)

Signed: ....
(signature of authorized official)

Place: ....

Date: ....

(seal or stamp of the Authority, as appropriate)

Signed: ....
(signature of Authorized official)

Place: ....

Date: ....

(seal or stamp of the Authority, as appropriate)

Signed: ....
(signature of authorized official)

Place: ....

Date: ....

(seal or stamp of the Authority, as appropriate)

NOTE: An intermediate survey may take the place of a mandatory annual survey where the relevant provisions of 1.5.2.1.3 and 1.5.2.1.4 are complied with.

ENDORSEMENT FOR INTERMEDIATE SURVEYS

THIS IS TO CERTIFY that at an intermediate survey required by 1.5.2.1.3 of the International Code for the Construction and Equipment of Ships Carrying Liquefied Gases in Bulk, the ship was found to comply with the relevant provisions of the Code.

Signed: . . . .
(signature of authorized official)

Place: . . . .

Date: . . . .

(seal or stamp of the Authority, as appropriate)

Signed: . . . .
(signature of authorized official)

Place: . . . .

Date: . . . .

(seal or stamp of the Authority, as appropriate)

Continued list of products to those specified in section 3, and their conditions of carriage.

Products	Conditions of carriage (tank numbers, etc.)

Date . . . .
     (as for Certificate)   *(signature of official issuing the Certificate and/or seal of issuing Authority)*

ATTACHMENT 2 TO THE INTERNATIONAL CERTIFICATE OF FITNESS FOR THE CARRIAGE OF LIQUEFIED GASES IN BULK

TANK PLAN (specimen)

Name of ship: . . . .

Distinctive number or letters: . . . .

◁————————————Cargo area————————————▷

Diagrammatic tank plan to be drawn in this area

Date . . . .
    (as for Certificate)   *(signature of official issuing the*
                                         Certificate and/or seal of issuing
                                              Authority)

Resolution MSC.30(61)
(adopted on 11 December 1992)

Adoption of amendments to the International Code for the Construction and Equipment of Ships Carrying Liquefied Gases in Bulk (IGC Code)

THE MARITIME SAFETY COMMITTEE,

RECALLING Article 28(b) of the Convention on the International Maritime Organization concerning the functions of the Committee,

RECALLING ALSO resolution MSC.5(48), by which the Committee adopted the International Code for the Construction and Equipment of Ships Carrying Liquefied Gases in Bulk (IGC Code),

RECALLING FURTHER article VIII(b) and regulation VII/11.1 of the International Convention for the Safety of Life at Sea (SOLAS), 1974, as amended, concerning the procedure for amending the IGC Code,

BEING DESIROUS of keeping the IGC Code up to date,

HAVING CONSIDERED, at its sixty-first session, amendments to the Code proposed and circulated in accordance with article VIII(b)(i) of the SOLAS Convention,

1.   ADOPTS, in accordance with article VIII(b)(iv) of the SOLAS Convention, amendments to the Code, the text of which is set out in annex* to the present resolution;

2.   DETERMINES, in accordance with article VIII(b)(vi)(2)(bb) of the Convention, that the amendments shall be deemed to have been accepted on 1 January 1994 unless, prior to that date, more than one third of the Contracting Governments to the SOLAS Convention or Contracting Governments the combined merchant fleets of which constitute not less than 50% of the gross tonnage of the world's merchant fleet, have notified their objections to the amendments;

3.   INVITES Contracting Governments to note that, in accordance with article VIII(b)(vii)(2) of the SOLAS Convention, the amendments shall enter into force six months after their acceptance in accordance with paragraph 2 above;

---

* See page 1.

4.   REQUESTS the Secretary-General, in conformity with article VIII(b)(v) of the SOLAS Convention, to transmit certified copies of the present resolution and the text of the amendments contained in the annex to all Contracting Governments to the SOLAS Convention;

5.   FURTHER REQUESTS the Secretary-General to transmit copies of the resolution and its annex to Members of the Organization, which are not Contracting Governments to the SOLAS Convention.